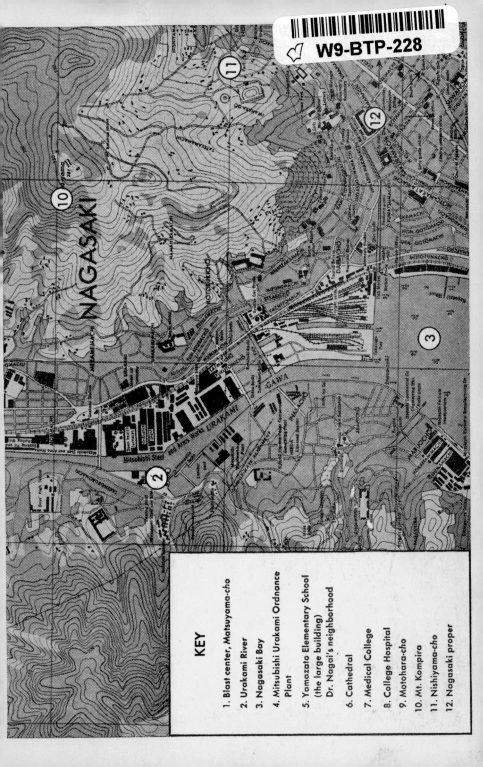

W9-BTP-228

KEY

1. Blast center, Matsuyama-cho
2. Urakami River
3. Nagasaki Bay
4. Mitsubishi Urakami Ordnance Plant
5. Yamazato Elementary School (the large building) Dr. Nagai's neighborhood
6. Cathedral
7. Medical College
8. College Hospital
9. Motohara-cho
10. Mt. Kompira
11. Nishiyama-cho
12. Nagasaki proper

which Nagai has edited so that they give a complete, interlocking picture of the bombing in all its aspects, rival in reportorial vividness the Hersey account of Hiroshima, with an added authenticity that comes only from direct, first-person narration.

The cumulative effect of these eight stories, however, goes beyond a portrayal of incomputable suffering and death. In his final chapter Nagai points this out; he for the first time draws the attention of the world to an aspect of atomic bombing which has been forgotten in the concern over physical effects:

The bomb that struck Nagasaki on August 9, 1945, was Atom Bomb Number Three. The fissures which then appeared throughout the blast center have not yet disappeared, four years after. I am not talking about cracks in the ground. I am talking about the invisible chasms which appeared in the personal relationships of the survivors. These rents in the ties of friendship and love have not closed up with the passage of time; on the contrary, they seem to be getting wider and deeper. They are cracks and fissures in the mutual esteem of fellow citizens . . . of all the damage the atom bomb did to Nagasaki, they are by far the cruelest. . . .

It is this spiritual wreckage, which the visitor to Nagasaki's wastes does not see, that is indeed beyond repair.

WE OF NAGASAKI

The Japanese Works of
TAKASHI NAGAI
(*Published during 1948 and 1949*)

Genshi-byo Kanja no Shuki
> *'Memoirs of a Radiation Casualty'*

Horobinu Mono o
> *'They Who Will Never Die'*—an autobiography

Kono Ko o Nokoshite
> *'Leaving One's Children Behind'—letters instructing the author's children in the spiritual principles which should guide their lives after his death*

Rozario no Kusari
> *'The Chain of the Rosary'*

Itoshigo yo
> *'My Dear Children'*

Nagasaki no Kane
> *'The Bell of Nagasaki'—on the bombing as experienced by the author and his colleagues at the Nagasaki Medical College*

Genshi-un no Shita ni Ikite
> *'Survivors Under the Atomic Clouds'—compositions on their experiences by the children of the Yamazato Elementary and Junior High School, edited by the author*

WE OF NAGASAKI

THE STORY OF SURVIVORS
IN AN ATOMIC WASTELAND

By TAKASHI NAGAI translated by
Ichiro Shirato and Herbert B. L. Silverman

DUELL, SLOAN AND PEARCE
New York

COPYRIGHT, 1951, BY

DUELL, SLOAN & PEARCE, INC.

I

*All rights reserved, including
the right to reproduce this book
or portions thereof in any form.*

PRINTED IN THE

UNITED STATES

OF AMERICA

A NOTE ON NAMES

Japanese names commonly occur in reverse order; that is to say, Takashi Nagai would be "Nagai Takashi" in Japan. In this book it has seemed preferable to employ the accepted English form. Furthermore, nearly all of the narrators, being Catholic, have taken an additional religious name; thus the author signs himself on the coverleaf of his manuscript "Poro (Paul) - Nagai Takashi," while the inscription on his wife's grave reads "Marina - Nagai Midori." Again, to simplify, the religious names have been dropped throughout.

To avoid confusion arising from the extensive and complicated family connections of the various narrators, each chapter is preceded by a short note on the narrator and on his or her relationship to those mentioned in the subsequent text.

INTRODUCTION

This book * was written expressly for translation into English; it has not appeared in Japan, although certain sections, in different form, were contained in earlier publications by the author, and were, in fact, the inspiration for the book as a whole. It is not only the first Japanese report on the atomic bombings to become available to Western readers, it is one of the few discussions of the moral after-effects of the bombings written by any Japanese since the war. Contemporary newspaper accounts and strictly technical papers on the atom bomb's effects there have of course been, but fiction and commentary in Japan are sparse, and none has gained a wide readership except Dr. Nagai's seven previous books.

In Japan Nagai is read certainly for his vivid reportorial detail—he himself was but a quarter-mile from

* Whose Japanese title is *Genshi Senjo Shinri*—literally, "Psychology of People on an Atomic Battlefield."

the blast-center when the Nagasaki bomb exploded—but perhaps more for the special emotional needs his works fill for many Japanese. He is clearly contriving out of the doctrine of his church—Nagai is a Roman Catholic—an adjustment to his new, bleak condition, as well as a rationale toward defeat and an attitude toward the conqueror. Even those who are not in accord with his religious philosophy are unquestionably able to experience, through reading him, a vicarious catharsis that is both an outlet for pain and an outlet for the various forms of survival-guilt which Nagai presents as the most formidable consequence of the bomb to the bombed.

Prior to 1946, Takashi Nagai did no professional writing. He was born in 1908 to a non-Christian family in Matsue, a town on the Japan Sea coast of Honshu, largest of the four main islands of Japan. His father was a doctor, and in 1928 Nagai entered medical school in Nagasaki. After graduation he remained at the College, teaching, and in 1940 was appointed assistant professor of radiology. Twice during this period he served as an army medical corpsman, in 1931 during the "Manchurian Incident," and again in 1932 during the "Shanghai Incident." He was also, in 1934, baptized in the Roman Catholic Church, and subsequently married Midori Moriyama of Nagasaki, whose ancestors had been among the early Japanese Christians.

Although Nagai was made a full professor at the Nagasaki Medical College in 1946, chronic leukemia, originally contracted in the radiology laboratories and aggravated by the conditions in wartime and postwar Japan, has subsequently prevented him from pursuing his profession. In 1948 his condition became critical and he was given the last rites. Since then there has been some improvement, but he remains bedridden. He lives with his son Makoto (now fifteen, the narrator of Chapter III) and his daughter Kayano (now nine, the narrator of Chapter II) in a one-room cabin built over the site of the house which, with his wife in it, was destroyed when the bomb fell. This home he calls *Nyokodo*, awkwardly translated as "Love-Thy-Neighbor-as-Thyself House."

In *We of Nagasaki* eight survivors of the bomb—five adults and three children, relatives and neighbors of the author—recount their individual experiences of the explosion, its aftermath, and its sequel in their own lives. In his editing Nagai has preserved entirely the plain, unsophisticated character of the narratives, while focusing each one in such a way as to point up the theme that a spiritual wreckage, more vast than the material, must result from atomic war.

The fact that the narrators are all Catholic provokes some inquiry into the history of Christianity in Japan and particularly around Nagasaki. The first recorded mission was that of St. Francis Xavier, who came to Japan in 1549 and is credited with having introduced Christianity. His and subsequent missions prospered, until by the start of the seventeenth century there were perhaps 300,000 * Christians in all Japan, of which possibly as many as one-half were concentrated in the Nagasaki area. From the very beginning Urakami, then a village, today a Nagasaki suburb and the locale of this book, was a chief Catholic center. As the sentiment of the Japanese rulers toward Christianity began to change sharply toward the end of the sixteenth century, Urakami in 1597 saw the crucifixion of twenty-six missionaries and native Christians—an event still commemorated by worldwide Catholicism with a mass each February 5th. In 1637–8 religious persecution reached

* According to *Japan Past and Present,* by Edwin O. Reischauer (New York, 1946).

a climax with the massacre of 37,000 Christian peasants in the Nagasaki area. Thereafter, for two and a half centuries, Christianity remained underground. As late as 1867–9 three thousand Christians were reported arrested in Nagasaki and exiled to other parts of Japan.

At the time of the bombing in 1945, the population of Nagasaki was about 250,000. Some 10,000 Catholics, four per cent of the total figure, lived in Urakami. The Cathedral there, the largest in East Asia, seated six thousand. The suburb had a long tradition of Catholicism, nurtured by centuries of concealment and persecution. Almost all of Nagai's relatives and neighbors were Catholic. From these circumstances, therefore, the particular religious feeling—at first startling in a book by a Japanese—can be understood.

Finally, a geographical note. Nagasaki lies about fifteen miles from the end of the Hizen-hanto, the large southward-curving peninsula which juts from the northwestern corner of the island of Kyushu. An indentation in this peninsula forms Nagasaki Bay, along whose shore the city extends, roughly twelve square miles in area. Flowing southward into the bay at the northwestern end of Nagasaki is the Urakami River, along both of whose banks lies the highly industrialized suburb of Urakami, target of the bomb. Here were located the various buildings repeatedly referred to in the narratives: the homes of Dr. Nagai and his neighbors, with the Yamazato Elementary School (whose shelter plays such an important part) nearby; then, some three hundred yards to the southeast, the Catholic Cathedral, the Nagasaki Medical College, and the College Hospital (where the author was at the time of the explosion), extending at 150-yard intervals in a straight north-south line; and finally, several hundred yards north of Nagai's community, across a bend in the river, the huge Mitsubishi Urakami Ordnance Plant, where many of those from the district worked.

The bomb exploded on August 9, 1945, at an altitude of fifteen hundred feet over Matsuyama, the riverfront section of Urakami. The area it leveled ran two miles north-to-south, and about seven-tenths of a mile from east to west. The hills which surround Nagasaki were effective in preventing the blast from reaching a number of outlying villages, among them Koba, three miles northeast of Urakami and separated from it by Mount Kawabira; this was the hamlet where Nagai and his wife had a summer home, which served as a refuge for their

Urakami neighbors after the bomb fell. A tributary of the Urakami River (the stream referred to in Chapters II, III, and IV) rises at Koba, and along it a road runs, skirting the northern base of Mount Kawabira and passing through the villages of Kawabira and Topposui, where the "Sojiro incident" took place and where the mill mentioned in Chapter V was located. The district of Nishiyama, like Koba, was protected by an intervening mountain—Mount Kompira—from the major effects of the bomb, though the narratives mention this area as having experienced a strange rain of oil.

CONTENTS

WE OF NAGASAKI

CHAPTER I

The Atomic Mentality

What would the world be like in an atomic war of extended duration?

Some will answer, "We know what it would be like. The scientists and the writers have already drawn us adequate pictures of what may be expected."

But these pictures have never been complete. The experts have shown cities demolished and fields laid waste; they have talked about genetic effects and about radiation sickness. But very little has been said about *people* in an atomic war, *as people.*

3

The mentality of human beings is not going to be simply a wartime mentality—a familiar phenomenon, somewhat intensified.

They are going to flee their cities and abandon their civilizations. They are going to dig into hillsides and hole up in mountain caves like beasts. They are going to go mad of fear without surcease.

And the fact that they survived when friends and loved ones died; that, when faced by the grim choice, they left these to perish that their own skins might be saved; that they loved not their neighbor—will press ever down upon their souls.

CHAPTER II

Kayano Nagai's Story

The narrator, Kayano Nagai, is the daughter of Dr. Nagai, and the younger sister of Makoto Nagai (who narrates Chapter III). Four years old at the time of the bombing, she was staying at the Nagai country home in Koba with Makoto and an old nurse. Among those she mentions in the course of her story are:

The sisters Fujie Urata Matsumoto (who narrates Chapter IV) and Tatsue Urata (who narrates Chapter V), cousins of Kayano's mother, Midori Moriyama Nagai; and the Uratas' mother, "Granny Take."

Three other cousins, the sisters Sadako (narrator of Chapter VII) and Sayoko Moriyama, and their brother Takeo.

The schoolteacher Hatsuji Tagawa, his sons Shinji, Naoshi, and Toshibumi, and his daughter Hiroko.

Ritsuko Miwa, another cousin, who plays an important part in Chapter IV.

Masanori Fukabori, brother of Satoru Fukabori, who narrates Chapter IX.

Akiko Tsuchie (see also Chapter V).

5

I can remember when I was little, but mostly bad things; I mean, mostly times when I was scared and things like that. The year I was born the war began. The whole time I was little there were air raids all the time. It was awful but anyhow I had my Mummy then, so it was so nice; I was so happy.

I saw the atom bomb. I was four then. I remember the cicadas chirping. The atom bomb was the last thing that happened in the war and no more bad things have happened since then, but I don't have my Mummy any more. So even if it isn't bad any more, I'm not happy.

It's very different now from the way it used to be before the atom bomb. Everything is different except maybe our stone fence, that's the only thing that's not different.

I used to live in a big house. There were lots of rooms on the second floor. There was a tree with red camellias on it in back of the house. I could touch the flowers if I felt like it—all I had to do was just put my hand out the window. All around us were houses. In front of us, I mean through the front windows, I could see lots and lots of houses, and on the other side of them was a hill with the big red cathedral on it, and after that was another hill with the college where my Daddy used to work.

Downstairs we had lots of rooms too. My Daddy had so many, many books. My Mummy used to make my clothes on the machine and my brother's too. I remember the funny noise it used to make—it used to go whirrr! Mummy used to make all kinds of *tempura* * in the kitchen, potato *tempura* for a snack in the afternoon and sardine *tempura* for dinner, and she knew how to make delicious *tempura* out of pine needles and maple leaves too—they were good!; we ate those during the war.

I used to have many friends, too. Across the street, Masanori Fukabori was my friend and Naoshi and Toshibumi and Shinji Tagawa were my friends too—the Tagawas were next door to the Fukaboris; and my friend Akiko lived down the hill at the Tsuchies'; and Ritsuko Miwa was my friend at the Moriyamas'—they lived in back of us. They were all my friends and we used to play house sometimes and sometimes quarrel.

We always had lots of pretty flowers in our garden. I remember one afternoon when I was playing out in

* Vegetables or fish wrapped in dough and fried in deep oil.

7

the garden and Daddy came along. He had on his pretty suit and he was carrying his black briefcase. I ran up to him and he let me hold his briefcase and I called to my mother that Daddy was home. Mummy came out, she was smiling, and she said, "Your bath is ready." We went inside and Daddy and Brother and I took turns at the tub. I got in first and I said, "Ooeee! It's hot!," so Mummy went out to the well and brought back a pail of cold water and poured it into the tub. That made it just right for me, but when it came Brother's turn he said it wasn't hot enough, so Mummy had to stir up the fire and heat up the water again. I remember she got all wrapped up in the smoke and it made her eyes full of tears but she laughed anyway. When I touched Daddy he felt very fat.

There were so many times we had air raids. There got to be more and more of them—they began coming every day, but that was near the end of the war. The sirens used to be very loud, and we used to run around and get all excited at my house, and so did they next door and across the road, too. Mummy used to put heavy clothes on me and make me wear an air-raid cap. It was stuffed with cotton so that I could wear the heavy helmet without being hurt. She made us all carry knapsacks on our backs and put on our leather shoes * to run faster; and then she took us to the air-raid shelter. The shelter was an awful old place. It was always dark and damp and full of mosquitoes and we always got all bitten up, and there wasn't any room to play either —we never had any fun there.

The air-raid headquarters were at the school, and they used to ring the school bells, "Cling-clang! Cling-clang!," just before the planes were over our heads, so that everybody would know to stay in the shelter. Then the anti-aircraft guns used to go "Pum-pum-pum!"— my brother told me that was the anti-aircraft guns—and the bombs!—what an awful noise *they* made! They went "Da-don! Da-don! Da-don!" when they hit the ground. But I had a good time, it was nice because Mummy held me tight. When we were home, not in the air-raid shelter, she was too busy.

Lots of bombs fell near our house, so Daddy and Mummy decided to send me and Makoto to Koba. We had a house in Koba up on the mountain, there was an old lady there who kept house for us. So Mummy took us and left us with the old lady, and she used to come and visit us.

* Ordinarily children wore wooden clogs, or *geta*.

9

Then one day Mummy came to see us and that was the last time. She brought me some *mompe* * she had just made for me. All of a sudden we heard the air-raid sirens, so Mummy stayed with us a while. Then we heard the all-clear. Mummy was in a hurry to get back to Urakami and see if everything was all right, so she ran down the hill; but first she patted me on the head and promised me, "Next time I come I'll bring you some *tempura* and *manju*.† "

Next morning I felt lonesome for Mummy and Makoto did too, so we decided to go down to Urakami. Brother picked some plums for Mummy, she always used to like plums, and we were just going to start out when the air-raid sirens started again and we couldn't go—we were so disappointed.

Brother said he was going swimming, so he went down to the river and I started to play house on the *engawa*.‡ The cicadas were making a lot of noise and I hadn't had my lunch yet.

---

* Loose-fitting cotton knickers which tie at the ankles; these were worn originally by peasant women, and became especially popular during the war among the general public.

† Bean-jam buns.

‡ A corridor along the outside of most Japanese houses, upon which most of the rooms open. It is normally on the sunny side and often serves as a sun porch.

10

All of a sudden there was a great big flash, like lightning. I didn't know what it was—I was so surprised! Then there was a big noise, then a big strong wind came and pushed me. I was scared. I got on the floor and stayed there with my hands over my ears.

First I didn't dare to, but after a while I took my hands away from my ears and I couldn't hear the cicadas —they weren't chirping any more. Then I opened my eyes and got up and, oh, my!, what an awful thing I saw!

From the other side of the big green mountain there was a great big red thing like a tree sticking up into the sky. It was a big big tree made out of fire. The top of it kept opening and opening and it looked as if it was alive. It kept swelling and swelling and it went up and up, higher and higher, like smoke from a chimney, all the way up to the sky, and then it kept going up even higher, right past the sky. First it was all red but it began to be different colors—oh, so bright! It made my eyes hurt!

I kept watching it and after a while the colors weren't so bright any more, then the whole thing turned grayish and spread all over the sky.

Just then my brother came running up the hill from

11

the river without any clothes on. He was all excited and he said, "My goodness! What was that? That plane must have crashed into the sun!"

Sure enough, the sun wasn't shining—I looked up at it through the awful cloud and it was the color of a dead thing.

Everything got dark, almost as dark as night, and cold, too, and pieces of burnt paper kept falling down out of the sky. Brother took hold of my hand and took me behind the sasanqua tree in back of the house. There were lots of pretty strawberries all around; they were nice and ripe but we didn't feel like eating any.

We could see lots of black smoke going up on the other side of the mountain, from under where the cloud was. Makoto said the cloud was over Urakami. He said, "Urakami's been hit!" The two of us stood there watching over the top of the mountain. After a little while the cicadas chirped again.

Then it began to rain and the raindrops were big and greasy. They made dark spots on my dress, and the taro leaves were covered all over with greasy drops sticking to them. We were afraid of such a funny kind of rain so we went back indoors.

12

The house was something awful inside! The *shoji* *
were down and all Mummy's boxes and *chochin* † had
been knocked off the shelves. Brother turned the switch
to make the radio play but it was dead. He said, "I
wonder what happened to our house?"

I said, "Oh, Mummy will come and tell us everything
soon." So we went outside and stood under the shaddock tree in the garden and waited and waited but
Mummy didn't come.

Cousin Fujie Urata and Cousins Sadako and Sayoko
and Takeo Moriyama came along in the evening with
Ritsuko. I asked, "Where is Mummy? Is she coming
later?," and Cousin Fujie said, "What! Isn't she here?"
Then she just took me in her arms and cried and cried.
She could hardly stop. When she did, she said, "Kaya-
chan,‡ after tonight you'll sleep next to Cousin Fujie,
shall we, Kaya-*chan*?"

That was nice. I liked Cousin Fujie. I said, "Oh,
good, that's nice!"

---

* The sliding doors, made of translucent paper pasted on wooden lat-
tices, which separate the rooms from the *engawa*, and may also be used to
divide one large room into two smaller ones.
† The familiar "Japanese lanterns."
‡ The suffix -*chan* is an expression of endearment.

13

Ritsuko just went and lay right down on the *tatami*.*
She wouldn't get up and play with me, she just stayed
there. Cousin Sadako put her arms around her but she
kept crying, "Oo, it hurts! Mama! It hurts!," but nobody knew where her mother was. Ritsuko had pur-
plish marks all over her. Cousin Sadako said a pile of
dirt had fallen on Ritsuko in the air-raid shelter and
buried her. How awful for poor Ritsuko! Brother gave
her and Takeo some plums but they didn't eat any—
they just kept asking for "Water, water"; that was all
they wanted.

Then Cousin Fujie went down to Urakami again. She
said she had to go and try to find old Granny Take.
And then, after she had left, Brother said, "I'm going
to go and get Mummy," and he went out and Cousin
Sadako went along with him.

Then the sun went down but the sky was still red
over the mountain, from the fire, not from the sunset.
After dark Makoto and Sadako came back, but Mummy
wasn't with them. Sadako lit a candle because the
lights weren't working. Then we all said our prayers;
but we didn't fall asleep for a long time.

* Matting made of latticed weeds stuffed with straw. The wood floors of
Japanese houses are usually covered with these mats.

In the morning the sky was all blue again over the mountain and the sun was strong again, too.

Early in the morning Cousin Fujie said she was going back to Urakami, and she told us children to go to the shelter under the shaddock tree if there were any planes. Lots of planes * did come, and we stayed in the shelter most of the time. Brother and I were waiting and waiting for Mummy. I couldn't understand why she didn't come and bring the *tempura* and *manju* the way she'd promised. I wondered if it was because of the fire in Urakami, but I didn't care about the *tempura* and *manju* if only Mummy would come soon. Mummy always wore dark clothes, and we always were able to see her coming along the road from a long way off. We saw lots of people, but they were all somebody else. After a while Cousin Fujie came along. She said, "Kaya-*chan*, poor little thing!," and she began to cry.

Then Cousin Tatsue Urata showed up and she also said, "Poor little Kayano," and began to cry.

I couldn't understand why Mummy wasn't with them. I said, "Where is Mummy? Wasn't she home? Couldn't you find her?" Then I asked, "What about Granny Take?" But they kept on crying.

* These were photo-reconnaissance planes.

15

"Everybody's dead, everybody, Kaya-*chan*," Fujie said.

Ritsuko was still crying, the same as yesterday. "Mama! Where are you? I want Mamma! Oo, I hurt!"— that was all she kept saying, all the time. Ritsuko's mother was dead, Cousin Fujie said.

A little after, Mr. Tagawa, the teacher, came along with Shinji and Naoshi. Mrs. Tagawa was dead and Toshibumi and Hiroko were dead too.

I said, "I guess everybody is dead in Urakami, aren't they? Is that what everybody does in Urakami?"

Then they all got down on their knees together and began to say the prayer of the rosary.

After that night and one more night, at last Daddy came along. It was in the morning. He had lots of nurses and doctors with him. Makoto and I were afraid to go near Daddy; his head was all wrapped in bandages and the bandages were stiff and his clothes were stiff too from blood, I mean blood that had dried up. Daddy's face was pale and his eyes looked *so* bright! What a sight he was! It scared Brother so when he saw Daddy looking like that, that he got all excited and let go of a cicada that he was holding.

Daddy had a queer kind of look on his face when he

16

saw Brother and me. He looked at us in a strange kind of way. He had a can of peaches in his pocket and he took it out and gave it to us.

The house was full of the smell of medicine from Daddy and the other doctors and the nurses. They rested a while and then they all went out again. Some of them could hardly walk, and took canes along to lean on. They were going out to visit wounded people, there were so many, many wounded people! That thing that had looked like a red tree sticking up in the sky had killed and wounded lots and lots of people, Daddy said. Daddy said it was no ordinary cloud, it was an atomic cloud.

What an awful thing it was!

Ritsuko died. Before she died, she coughed up a lot of blood.

Takeo also coughed up a lot of blood and he died too.

Every day lots of people died every place.

Then we heard that Japan had lost the war. Daddy and everybody cried out loud just like children when they heard it. Daddy said I didn't have to hide in the air-raid shelter any more when I saw a plane, because the war was over and the planes weren't going to kill us any more. I was glad, because I didn't want to die like Ritsuko and get all cold and be wrapped up in a straw mat and be carried to the graveyard.

Daddy told me that that was what ended the war—the atomic cloud. So I guess the atomic cloud was even stronger than the war.

My Daddy got very sick and was almost going to die; he lost lots of his blood and he had a great fever. Brother and I kept saying the prayer of the rosary for him and that made him well again. We wouldn't know what to do if Daddy died.

In the fall, Daddy and Brother and I all went back to Urakami in an automobile. It was when the fruit on the shaddock tree was beginning to get ripe. Urakami was a very different kind of place. There wasn't anything left—our house, or the camellia tree, or the garden, or Mummy's sewing machine, or Daddy's books, or my picture-books, or the kitchen where my Mummy used to make *tempura,* or the swing Brother and I used to swing on, or the telephone, or my slippers, or anything. And there weren't any of my friends either —Masanori, or Isamu, or Cousin Hatsuko, or any of them, and old Mrs. Fukitani was gone too, and so was Mrs. Tsujimoto and the cathedral and Granny Take, and my mother.

It was all gone. I couldn't understand why, so I asked, "Why is everything gone, Daddy? Why is it?"

Daddy said, "It's all on account of the war." So I said, "Does a war always make everything go away?" Daddy said, "Yes, it certainly does," so I asked him, "Why does it?"

Daddy didn't answer me so I didn't understand.

We had a little place like a box, made out of some logs and some sheets of tin and our old stone fence, and that's what we used for a house. It was so small that when we all went to sleep we were very crowded. Once Brother said, "It's crowded, but it's warm," and I said, "Yes, it's warm but when we're asleep you always kick me, and that hurts."

All my friends were gone and there was only Makoto to play with me. Daddy made me a doll out of a wine jug.

Soon lots of *Haro-san* * came to Urakami. They came

* *Haro* is a Japanese attempt to pronounce "Hello." The suffix -*san* is an honorific meaning, approximately, "Mr." Thus the American troops were the "Mr. Hellos."

19

along in jeeps. Daddy told me they were marines and lots of them were college students. They were all very nice to us and they had very good manners, and whenever we said "Haro," they always used to say "Haro" right back to us and smile at us. They used to give us chocolate and chewing gum, they used to give us all they had so they never had any left for themselves.

Later that year there was a big funeral service for all the dead on the cathedral grounds; the cathedral was ruined. The service was for eight thousand dead people. The relatives of the dead people stood in rows holding white crosses, eight thousand crosses. I held a cross with my mother's name on it. There were more crosses than people at the service. It made everybody cry. There were bishops in purple robes and lots of priests, also many nuns dressed all in black. When we sang the hymns everybody sang in a loud voice and everybody's tears dried.

Afterward we went to visit Mummy's grave, where my Daddy had buried her ashes. There was a little stone Daddy had put there and we set up the white cross I carried at the funeral service.

That was four years ago. Daddy has been sick in bed ever since. He's lost a lot of weight and he's so thin now. But me, I am getting very big and tall. Cousin Fujie says I'm getting to look the way my mother used to. I'm always peeking in the mirror to see.

My mother's grave doesn't get any bigger or any smaller. Whenever I go and visit her, the stone and the cross just stand there. Now I can read what Daddy wrote on the cross four years ago, when he put it on the grave: *Marina - Nagai Midori. Died August 9th, 1945.*

CHAPTER III

Makoto Nagai's Story

The narrator is Nagai's son Makoto, ten at the time of the bombing and living out in Koba with his sister Kayano (see Chapter II). His mother's cousin Fujie Urata Matsumoto, mentioned in Chapter II, appears again here.

I was ten. We were staying at the cottage in Koba and I was down at the river swimming.

All of a sudden there was an airplane. It came from down the river. I looked up at the sky. I was at the bottom of the valley so I could see only a narrow strip of sky between the hillsides. A little way downstream there was a farmer standing alongside a rice paddy. Suddenly there was an awful light in the sky, toward Urakami. I just dived head-first into the water. When I came up, the farmer had fallen into the paddy, he was so surprised. From down the river came a noise like thunder. It was a terrific rush of wind. The leaves were torn off all the trees and came racing along. My

22

pants that I had left on a rock were blown along with the leaves.

It was getting dark and cold very fast. I thought an airplane must have crashed into the sun. Without anything on I started running up the hill toward the cottage. Somebody I couldn't see shouted at me from behind some bushes:

"What the devil are you doing? Hide! Quick! They'll spot you!"

I ran and got under a taro. The big leaves hid me completely. But I was worried about my little sister Kayano. I picked a taro leaf and held it over my head and ran to the house that way.

Everything was smashed. The pots had been blown off the stove. Kayano was all right but she was very excited. She was watching something over Mount Kawabira.

"Brother!," she yelled, "Look! Look! Over there!" I looked toward the mountain, where she was pointing.

What a sight! The biggest thing I ever saw, the biggest that ever was, was sticking way up into the sky from the other side of the mountain. It was like a cloud but it was like a pillar of fire too. It looked hard and soft and alive and dead all at the same time, and beautiful

23

and ugly, too, all at once. The light it sent out was all the colors of the rainbow. It almost blinded me with the glare. It kept getting taller and taller all the time, and wider and wider, twisting and rolling around just like smoke from a chimney. It was growing from the top, I mean, the top was getting pushed up from inside. Then the top began to spread out, so that it looked like an umbrella opening up.

You might say the thing was a sort of a cloud-fountain, I mean a fountain sending up clouds instead of water.

Kayano said it was all red when she first saw it and she said it had a shape like a tree, but by the time I saw it, it was very swollen and beginning to get whitish.

Where we were, we were about three miles away from it. The sun looked brownish like a chocolate cracker.

I began to be worried about my mother because the thing was in the direction of Urakami. I was just burning up inside, I was so worried. I couldn't stand it. I ran back down to the river and jumped right into the water to cool off.

Then I saw Cousin Fujie running down the hill. She had been working up in the millet patch. She shouted to me that she was going to Urakami and kept on running, all sweaty and red in the face. She had a jug of tea in her hand.

After a few minutes I saw something coming up the road along the river that looked like a parade of roast chickens. Some of them kept asking for "Water! Water!"

I wasn't burning up any more. I shivered. I ran back to the cottage.

I would rather blind myself than ever have to see such a sight again!

From that time to the end of the war, everybody seemed to be going crazy. Even when there weren't any planes or anything some people were very nervous and running around all the time, and some were scared and wouldn't budge out of their shelter. Some people got very jumpy, that is, they would get angry for no reason. Some didn't do things they should have, like their job and so on; and some did lots of senseless things they needn't have. There were some people that were always dropping things from nervousness and some couldn't remember anything—names and numbers and things like that. Many people had one eye on the sky all the time—they couldn't pay any attention to what they were doing, and they hardly heard you when you spoke. Life got all mixed up.

There were all sorts of rumors going around. Some people said that next time the enemy was going to use another new weapon even worse than the atom bomb. They didn't know when or where it was going to be used or what it was going to be like, but they were already so scared they were afraid even to pick up a piece of paper—they were afraid it might be poisoned. One order came out that we were not to get friendly with strangers because, on account of the new weapon, spies had landed along the beach and saboteurs had dropped by parachute in the hills. In church we had always learned that one should "aid travelers in distress," but nobody paid any attention to that now. In fact, there were some poor lost travelers who had asked children for directions, but the children did not tell them how to get where they were going—they just ran and reported them to the police and got rewards for it.

There were lots of things we did that broke the rules we had learned in church and at school. And the way we talked, too. People said, "It's a great sin to kill anybody, but if you can say that it's right to kill so many thousands of people, then anything is all right, no matter how bad." People could find excuses for almost anything. For instance, people said that anything anybody found belonged to whoever picked it up, so when they found anything they just kept it.

There were many farmers who ate their cows and chickens. They said, "Let's have a good time while we're here on earth, we won't be much longer—the atom bomb means it's all up with the world." Then peace was declared, and they were in a fix because they didn't have their cows and their chickens any more to get milk and eggs from or to pull their plows. So this was one more way the atom bomb upset people's ways of living.

And it wasn't only the farmers either. Most people just began watching out for themselves; they gave up their jobs or whatever they were supposed to be doing and headed into the mountains with their families. Soon there weren't any more people living the regular way—I mean, living together in families and families living together in neighborhoods, and lots of neighborhoods making up the city, and so on, like civilized people.

Everybody seemed to be finding all kinds of excuses

for being selfish—they seemed to think it was the right way to be. They began figuring out how they could call their selfish acts something else; how they could give their selfish acts some nicer name.

When the war stopped my father and little sister and I went back to Urakami—although there wasn't much left of it. One day in October an order from the school was posted: "All pupils of Yamazato Grade School will assemble immediately in the school yard!" I went right to school. There were three teachers and thirty pupils in the yard. Twenty-five teachers and about twelve hundred pupils had died. Another teacher and about three hundred pupils didn't turn up; they were out sick on account of wounds or atomic sickness. There had been about sixty of us in my class, but only four turned up. My own teacher was too overcome to speak. He just looked at us and dismissed us. The school looked like an old baker's oven. There was still lots of charred wood left on the playground from the cremations almost two months ago.

There was one family—the kind that had always had a reputation for being interested only in themselves—

that had stayed in the country all through the war on some excuse or other. As soon as the war stopped, they came back to town safe and sound. They had taken almost everything they owned with them so they brought it all back in good condition. They claimed that the reason they hadn't supported the war was that they hadn't believed in it. They believed in peace, they said. They said that we deserved to lose my mother—we had it coming to us for having been so stupid as to support the war. This got me mad.

Down to my father's generation, everybody considered bravery in battle something to be proud of. Everybody admired that and tried to be that way. It's up to my generation to make the courage to stop war something to be proud of—that's what *we* should admire and that's the way we should all try to be. It's all right to take the sword away from somebody who is trying to kill you with it but there is a good chance of a fight. What we want is to be brave enough and wise enough to let him keep the sword and still make him our friend.

CHAPTER IV

Fujie Urata Matsumoto's Story

Fujie Urata, who tells this story, was about thirty-five at the time of the bombing; after the war she married Sakutaro Matsumoto. When the explosion occurred she was working in a millet patch in Koba, and was thus spared. She, with her sister Tatsue (narrator of Chapter V), were first cousins of Midori Nagai, Dr. Nagai's wife. Other important relationships in this chapter are:

Take Urata (see also Chapter V), mother of Fujie and Tatsue and aunt of Midori Nagai.

Fujie's uncle, Suematsu Moriyama, and his daughters Sadako (narrator of Chapter VII), Sayoko, and his son Takeo (see also Chapter II).

Fujie's cousin Ritsuko Miwa (see also Chapter II), and Ritsuko's mother Shizuko Miwa, an older daughter of Suematsu Moriyama.

Kayano and Makoto Nagai, cousins (see Chapters II and III).

Fujie's cousin Sojiro Urata (see also Chapter VII), his son Takeyoshi, his wife Sami, and the latter's mother Mrs. Maruo.

Reiko Urata, another cousin.

Satoru Fukabori (narrator of Chapter IX), brother of Masanori Fukabori (see Chapter II).

Matsu Moriuchi (narrator of Chapter VI), aunt of Hatsue and Mataichi Tsujimoto, their daughter Kimiyo, and their son Isamu (see Chapter VI).

30

I was pulling up weeds in the rows of millet on the hillside at Koba, at a place three and a half miles from Urakami; Mount Kawabira stands in between. In Urakami we were neighbors of Dr. Nagai's, and if I had been at home at the time I certainly would have died. My old mother, Take Urata, who had stayed home to watch the house, was burned to death.

Suddenly I heard a loud roar overhead. It sounded as though a plane had just dropped its bombs and was flying away.

Here it comes, I thought.

There was a sudden flash of red light.

Then a flash of blue.

The red was bright enough to stun a person, but the blue!—it was so bright that not even the worst liar could have found the words to describe it.

That was all. There was a wind which blew away the weeds I had pulled up, but nothing else happened.*

What could these flashes be? . . .

I scanned the sky. Rising higher than high Kawabira, in the sky over Urakami, a puffy black smoke began

---

* The blast and the radiation were blocked by the intervening mountain.—*Auth.*

31

boiling up and up, filling that whole part of the sky. Kawabira seemed to divide the world in two, one part looking normal as ever and the other strange and terrible. I couldn't attend to my work. I sat down at the edge of the field. It was almost noon, so I ate some of the food I had brought. After about fifteen minutes a bawling, stark-naked child passed by along the road at the foot of the hill. He looked as though he had been swimming in the river and had had an accident.

Five minutes later a girl of about twenty came struggling along the road uphill from Urakami. Her clothes were in shreds and her hair in disorder. She seemed barely able to stay on her feet. I could hear her loud sobbing from where I sat on the side of the hill. Next a weeping schoolboy came along, his clothes in tatters also, and his face and hands black and swollen. I suddenly became anxious about my mother. I scrambled down the hillside and ran down the road toward Urakami.

As I came nearer to Urakami, I began to meet many injured people. They must have been workers from the arsenal,* young men and women, all of them naked, except that some still had their leather belts around

---

* The Mitsubishi Urakami Ordnance Plant.

their waists and on some the strings of their *mompe* still circled their ankles. They were stumbling along unsteadily, trying to escape behind Mount Kawabira, weeping crazily, forgetting even to be ashamed of their nakedness. Their faces, necks, and hands were blistered and on some of them I could see sheets of skin that had peeled right off and hung down flapping, all black with dust. The hair of the women was singed and frizzled. Many of these people had been wounded and were smeared with blood.

I tried to find out what had happened to them, and cried, "For heaven's sake, what is it! What's happened!" Always the same answer—"I don't know, all I saw was a sudden flash, then everything went to pieces!" Some just stared with blank expressions, unable to answer at all.

Sometimes one of them would stumble in the road and sprawl on his face, lying there without trying to get up.

I was carrying my jug of tea, so I ran from one to another making them drink a little. At the spring in Topposui I stopped to fill the jug with water. I was still about two miles from Urakami but already I could see many houses afire.

When I finally reached Urakami, about two hours after the big flash, I found everything in flames. I managed to get to a spot overlooking the Yamazato Elementary School. From here I could see that my own part of town was completely gutted. Everywhere, smoke rose from the embers. I tried to find the path to my house but the ground was covered with hot ashes and even if I had found it I couldn't have used it.

What had happened to my mother! I kept shouting and calling toward the house. There was no answer. I walked all around the neighborhood, wherever walking was possible. Finally I came to the school playground. There I found my cousin, Sadako Moriyama, who was fetching water, and her sister Sayoko and the two little ones, Takeo and Ritsuko, who were inside the shelter. Sadako had a dazed expression. The four children were just sitting there helpless, waiting for someone to come and take care of them.

What about my mother? . . . And my sister Tatsue? . . . And my cousin Midori, Dr. Nagai's wife? . . . And Sadako's family, the Moriyamas? . . . They were all on my mind. How could they have lived through this! Takeo and Ritsuko were shaking with sobs and

Ritsuko had cuts and bruises all over her body. I saw that they must be moved quickly. The whole sky was covered by a terrible cloud. It hid the sun completely and made the day like twilight.

We set out for Dr. Nagai's summer cottage on the hillside at Koba. I took Ritsuko on my back, and with Sadako pulling Takeo along we began to climb the road I had come down a while before.

As we walked Takeo kept doubling up and complaining, "My tummy hurts." He was getting weaker all the time. Sadako and Ritsuko were both feeling faint. It was a strange kind of weakness. I thought they must have been exposed to some sort of poisonous fumes.

When we finally reached the cottage, Makoto and Kayano, Dr. Nagai's children, were standing under the shaddock tree in the garden, looking as if they expected someone. They were overjoyed when they saw us and came running up.

"Where's Mummy?" Kayano asked immediately.

"What! Isn't she here yet?" I had taken it for granted. Makoto shook his head. He looked so lonely.

None of our relatives and neighbors from Urakami

were here yet. Could they all have died! I was half out of my mind. This time I was going to find my mother and bring her back. I hurried off to Urakami again.

But when I came alongside the spring in Topposui I found my cousin Sojiro Urata slumped in a heap on the ground, motionless as something carved. At first I did not recognize him. His face was burned and covered with black blisters and blood was trickling from his head. But there was something familiar about the shape of his mouth so I said to him, "Aren't you Cousin Sojiro?" He opened his eyes, narrow slits between swollen lids, as though he were awakening from sleep.

"Ah! Fujie? Take me to the church. Is it far? I want to confess to the father. I want the sacrament."

It was clear that death was crowding in on him. His right forearm was broken and horribly bent. It was gruesome. His shirt and trousers were in rags. He must have kept falling on the road. His whole body was caked with mud.

I had to find my mother but here was my cousin on the brink of death right before my eyes, craving pardon for his sins. I could not desert him. I decided I would first get him to the church in Koba, a mile and a half uphill, then return and find Mother.

36

He nibbled a little of the *mugimeshi* * I was carrying and drank from the spring. Then he said, "Get me some salt." I found some in a store near the spring and poured it in the palm of his hand. He licked it up hungrily.

I put a splint on his broken arm and hung it from his neck with a bandage. He was getting back a little of his spirit. Then I put my neck under his left arm, and with my right arm around his waist we began walking slowly. He was without strength. His legs wobbled so that I had to drag him while he hung on to me around the shoulders. As we struggled on he kept feeling faint and had to lie down in the road and rest. I spoke to him several times but he could only gasp. Each time we stopped to rest he would say, "I can't see. . . . Aren't we there yet? Is it far?"

Sojiro was a decent fellow, but in the army he had been a medical corps non-com and had also been a policeman in Shanghai, so in the past he had often swaggered around acting important. But now that he knew death's visit was near he had become very humble, earnestly clinging to the hand of God as he climbed the sloping road to the church.

"Is it still far?"

* Rice cooked with wheat.

How many times did I hear that question!

"Not very far. Keep your courage up!" How many times did I have to encourage him!

He looked as though his heart would collapse any minute. I was at my wit's end. On the road, here and there, sprawled the dead bodies of people who had struggled this far before they dropped. The road here ran along the stream and there were few houses. In two hours we covered about a mile, from Topposui to the little village of Kawabira. By a piece of luck I found a bicycle trailer in a store here, and I piled Sojiro into it. It was a great relief for him too, and he was overjoyed. The road now became a steep slope. It took more than my strength to get the trailer up the hill, and I had to ask help part of the way.

When we finally reached Koba it was on toward evening. I called from the foot of the stone steps leading up to the church and Father Shimizu came out, followed by Maruo, the cook, and others. They carried Sojiro inside.

Sojiro immediately asked for the last rites. Father Shimizu put on a short surplice and, with a stole about his shoulders, knelt at Sojiro's head and solemnly made the sign of the cross. . . . So Sojiro had received the

38

last sacrament. I had seen to it. I felt as if a load had been lifted from my shoulders.

Once again I hurried back down the road, pulling the empty trailer. At the shop I stopped to return it, but when I tried to continue toward Urakami the people there held me back. It was too dark to go looking for my mother now, they said. I would only be running into danger. In the sky over Urakami the horrible cloud was bright-red with the reflection of the burning town. As I stood there complete exhaustion suddenly came over my whole body. I suppose that my tension relaxed. Slowly I started back for the cottage in Koba.

How frightened and lonely the children were! The cottage was so still that I held my breath. With the power lines down outside, there was no light and the radio was dead. A red fire glowed in the *irori*.* Little Takeo Moriyama had fallen asleep, exhausted. Ritsuko was in pain from her injuries—she had been buried under mounds of earth—and she could not sleep.

"Mama! Mama!" She was racked with sobs. Her mother, Shizuko Miwa, was my cousin. Was she alive? I wondered. With the child calling for her so, surely she must be alive somewhere. Yet if she were safe and

* An open fireplace in the center of the sitting room.

sound she would certainly have come looking for them here long before now.

Makoto and Kayano made none of their usual noise and rumpus. They sat staring at the *irori*. "It's late," I said to them, "time to go to sleep," but they would not go. They kept their ears pricked up for the sound of footsteps outside . . . their father's or their mother's. Around the house the air was filled with the chirping of *suzumushi*.* The sound of footsteps would have stilled their noise, but when the night lifted and turned to day they had not stopped once.

The morning sky was clear. The cloud which had filled the sky over Urakami had drifted eastward. Somehow I felt a kind of hope; I had the feeling that it was over. I started out to look for my mother and sister.

Urakami was a hill of ashes. It had never been so hushed. It reminded me of the way deserts look in pictures, except that it was even more quiet than a desert. A desert is always bare of people, animals, and anything that grows but here, up to only yesterday, there had been houses and living creatures. In a single day these had disappeared.

In the ashes I could make out nothing moving or

---

* *Homæogryllus japonicus;* a cricket-like insect.

40

motionless. Up on one slope the cathedral was completely in flames, sending up a great red blaze. How still and solemn the whole scene looked under the morning sun! This was the only fire still burning in ancient Urakami. All the others had gone out.

My mother's bones were among the ashes of our house. I found her at the mouth of the air-raid shelter under the floor, consumed to such a little heap of bones. She must have heard the explosion and rushed to the shelter, where she was crushed. Since she was sixty-seven and had not been very well, she often had to lie down. She spent most of her time telling her beads and praying. That was her main business, but see how she departed this life! I decided I must find my sister Tatsue, and together we would gather her bones.

In the ruins of Ichitaro Yamada's house, next door to ours, I could see the bodies of four or five children alongside the body of an adult. Ichitaro himself had been drafted and was away in the army, and here was his family, wiped out. I would not want to see the look on his face when he came back.

My younger brother Masaichi was also away in the army. If he came back . . . he would say I had neglected Mother, he would blame me for having let her

41

die alone. I dreaded his anger, but my mother's ashes were more accusing still.

When I left the house yesterday my mother was asleep. The air-raid sirens had sounded during the night, and we had had to go to the community air-raid shelter. She was exhausted, so I let her sleep. Whenever I left the house I always said goodbye to her, but yesterday of all days I didn't want to wake her! . . . I left quietly without a word . . . Now I could hardly stand the pain of regret.

The pumpkin field in front of the house was blown clean. Nothing was left of the whole thick crop, except that in place of the pumpkins there was a woman's head. I looked at the face to see if I knew her. It was a woman of about forty. She must have been from another part of town—I had never seen her around here. A gold tooth gleamed in the wide-open mouth. A handful of singed hair hung down from the left temple over her cheek, dangling in her mouth. Her eyelids were drawn up, showing black holes where the eyes had been burned out. The head had come right off at the neck. There was not much blood. She had probably looked square into the flash and gotten her eyeballs burned, then the blast must have taken her head off

42

at the neck and sent it flying with the blood gushing out behind.

There was a big persimmon tree in the field, too big for one person to get his arms around. It had been snapped off at eye-level and blown through the air. From its position I guessed that the blast must have come from the direction of the Matsuyama section. Beside the stump lay the body of old lady Maruo. Her daughter Sami was squatting on the ground, in a trance, holding her child. Sami was Sojiro's wife.

"Sami!"

"What! Is it Fujie! You're alive? . . ."

"Come on! Pull yourself together! Don't you know Sojiro is at the church in Koba?"

"Is he alive?"

"I'm not sure. . . ."

"Is he dead, then? Tell me, Fujie! Or is he alive! *Is* he?"

"Go on, hurry over and find out. The father gave him the sacrament last night. I don't know what happened afterward."

"All right, I'm going. . . . I was pinned under the house but I got out all right, with the baby, but Takeyoshi, my eldest, was out chasing dragonflies and

43

he hasn't come back yet . . . I was just waiting. . . .
But how can I go to Sojiro? What about my mother's
body? And maybe Takeyoshi is alive, wandering around
some place! . . ."

Holding the baby, she stood up and sat down several
times, unable to make up her mind.

"Don't wait around thinking it over! There's no sense
in that. While you're thinking it over Sojiro may be
dying! Go on, hurry! Then come right back and we'll
attend to your mother. Anyway, there aren't any
coffins. We'll have to have one made in Koba and bring
it back. Come on, now; hurry up! If Takeyoshi is alive
he can get to Koba by himself. He's not an infant, he's
ten years old."

So together we offered prayers for her mother and
all the neighbors. Then she hurried off to the church
in Koba, carrying the baby.

In the wreck of Reiko Urata's house nearby I could
see a charred skeleton, sandwiched between the sink
and the stove. Could it be Reiko's mother? I wondered.

Next door to Reiko lived the Shibatas. The young
couple had been blown out onto the path behind the
house. Young Shibata had recently graduated from
medical school. They were good people and the wife

44

had been working in a school for the blind, paying her husband's expenses with what she earned. Finally he had gotten his degree and been appointed to Saga Hospital. They must have died together in happiness —right in the midst of packing to go to his new post in Saga.

Midori's bones were still in her kitchen, so I knew that Dr. Nagai had not come home yet. Because I knew that if he were alive he would want to bury her with his own hands, I let the bones lie where they were. Cousin Midori was the kind of person who is always full of energy. If she wasn't doing something she would get fidgety. But now she was at peace.

Across the way, in the ruins of Satoru Fukabori's house, were the remains of a large and a small skeleton. They would be Satoru's mother and baby brother. Next door was the wreck of Hatsuji Tagawa's house. Here too I could see charred bones. On the path between the Tanakas' and the Fukitanis' homes was a charred corpse. There were the remains of three skeletons in the ruins of Sadako Moriyama's house. In the garden behind the house, where he had been blown, Sadako's father, Suematsu, was sprawled on his face, dead. He had no external wounds, so he must have been slammed

45

against the ground and his insides squashed. I took off some of my clothes and covered him up. This was no time to try and take care of the body. I went over to the shelter in the schoolyard and there I saw Ritsuko's mother, Shizuko. She looked far gone—already her breathing was uneven. As soon as she saw me she asked, "Where's Ritsuko?"

"She's alive. She's in Koba."

She nodded, and I thought I saw a flicker of a smile in her blistered face.

Shizuko had been over to Motohara, about four hundred yards away, where a house was going up. She had been hired to do light work and odd jobs, and must have been there when the big flash came. But she was suffering so terribly I didn't try to ask questions. With the entire front of her body scorched she still had managed to crawl back to the school shelter. Probably thinking Ritsuko would be here, like any mother worried about her only child, she must have crawled the four hundred-odd yards from Motohara to the school grounds.

When I told her that Ritsuko was alive, she felt at peace. Immediately she went limp with exhaustion. "Look after Ritsuko, will you, Fujie? Take care of her!

46

Until my husband comes back from the war," she kept begging me.

After a few minutes she cried, "Get me some water!" I had filled my jug with tea before leaving Koba; I tried to make her drink some but her lips were so swollen that she could barely get her mouth open. Finally I thought of plucking a straw and making her suck the tea through it.

"Ah! That's good!" she said. The words seemed to come from the bottom of her heart.

I decided to go to the medical school and get Dr. Nagai. I started off for Yamazato-*cho* * but the ashes on the ground were still hot and I couldn't make any headway. There was nothing to do but return to the shelter. I had been gone ten minutes; when I got back, Shizuko was dead.

Everybody was dead, everybody I had come looking for. And I had expected I would be coming back to Koba today with all of them—I had been so keyed up, looking forward to the excitement. . . .

There in the school yard Mr. Tagawa was burying two children. He told me they were Kimiyo, the Tsujimotos' little girl, and his own second boy, Toshi-

* The suffix -*cho* means, approximately, "precinct."

47

bumi. Two of his children and old Auntie Matsu Mori-uchi were alive in the shelter. They seemed to be the last survivors in the entire *cho*. Yet some day the neighborhood would live and prosper again, I knew.

Enemy planes roared by overhead, one after another. I was tense, dreading still another great flash. I knew that there was supposed to be danger in an air raid only while the planes were directly overhead; if you were careful, you could avoid the bombs. But now I didn't know when or where another big flash might come.

If a war like this lasted very long we would go out of our minds if we survived at all. I suddenly felt terrified. I could not stay here in Urakami a minute longer. I just left my mother's body and the bodies of so many of my relatives and scurried off to Koba.

Makoto and Kayano Nagai were waiting under the shaddock tree. "Where's Mummy?" Kayano asked.

The two children were now motherless—but there they were, still standing under the shaddock, waiting for their mother who would never return.

I couldn't answer. Suddenly throwing my arms around Kayano I began to cry.

48

Makoto was holding a handful of plums. He must have picked them to give to his mother as soon as I brought her back.

Ritsuko was sleeping in Sadako's arms, but she kept waking. "Mama! Mama! Where is Mama?" she wept.

Sadako kept patting her back gently. "Go to sleep. Mama will come while you're sleeping. She'll bring something yum-yum. Go to sleep now, there's a good girl." The tot believed her. But Shizuko was lying there in the air-raid shelter, cold and dead.

Sadako was completely crushed when she saw me coming back alone. They were all dead—her father and mother, her brother and her sister. Telling her was like trying to spit out chestnut burrs. Sadako and Sayoko fell into each other's arms, weeping. All of a sudden they had found themselves orphans.

We were eight in the cottage and we had every one lost our mothers.

Just then Mr. Tagawa came along with two of his boys. They also had lost their mother the day before.

Near evening my sister Tatsue turned up safe and sound. For twenty-four hours I had been beside myself, running around everywhere looking for her, half out of my mind wondering whether she was dead or alive,

49

and here she calmly appears big as life and without a scratch. It was such a thrill and such a relief.

"Tatsue, you little fool!" I exploded. "What a time you've given me!"

"Fujie, you dunce! I'm the one who's been going crazy looking for you!"

We hugged, trembling with the joy of finding each other alive. The tears ran in floods.

"Mother—you know—"

But Tatsue had seen the ruins of the house. She stopped me. "Yes, I know, I know."

We both wept aloud.

Ritsuko kept wailing, "Mama! Oh Mama! Where's Mama?"

Little Kayano was only four, so when we told her her mother was dead she didn't cry—she didn't know what it meant. We tried to tell her what had happened but she only smiled and asked, "When is Mummy coming?"

In the evening Ritsuko began to have diarrhea. I couldn't remember giving her anything special to eat that might have upset her stomach. She seemed to have some strange sickness. Shizuko had begged me with her dying breath to take care of Ritsuko and her voice still rang in my ears. I must keep Ritsuko alive until her father came back from overseas.

Sadako and Sayoko were both stretched out limp, unable to sit up. They had a feeling like seasickness. It was different from just plain exhaustion. We knew it must have something to do with the bomb.

The second day after the bomb fell was still hot but the ashes had cooled so one could breathe much more easily. In Urakami planes came by overhead, one after another. There seemed to be no end to them. We knew that if another great flash came we would all be dead. When we heard the roar of an engine we didn't stop to look up—we just made a dash to take cover any place; but there was almost nothing left to hide in. There was hardly anything in sight still standing. We heard a rumor that the invasion troops of the Allies were off the coast of Kyushu. If they landed at Nagasaki now, what would happen to us! Our own defenses and our troops were destroyed; if tanks landed, what in heaven would become of us! After all we had suffered, to have to go through more now! . . . I felt I'd as soon be crushed to death quickly under a tank and have it over with.

Tatsue and I gathered our mother's bones and put them in a bucket. The sound they made dropping in reminded us of her cough. Mother had asthma and was always wheezing and hacking. Sometimes it was painful for her to breathe. But now she was rid of her pain.

We buried her in Akagi Cemetery. It was a lonely funeral, with just the two of us, huddled together and flattening ourselves on the ground every time a plane passed over. We set up a small gravestone, and as soon as it was over we hurried straight back to Koba, leaving the bodies of Shizuko and Uncle Suematsu.

Ritsuko had gotten weaker. Red spots had begun to break out all over her body and the diarrhea was worse. Medicine did her no good. She kept asking for water and wailing, "Mama, oh, where's Mama?" Sadako and Sayoko stayed with her all the time. They didn't know what to say to her—they couldn't lie and say that her mother was coming soon.

They both said they were feeling a little better but I could see that they did not have their strength back.

On the morning of the third day after the bomb nine or ten young men and women came along. They were all worn out with exhaustion and some could hardly walk without help. Their leader was a tall young man with his head and neck wrapped in thick bandages, stained with dried blood. It was Dr. Nagai, and his companions were the surviving members of the Department of Radiology of the Medical College, doctors and nurses. Their bandages smelled of blood. Seeing the way they looked made us all weep. Kayano and Makoto were so frightened that they tried to run away.

The doctor shouted, "Come on, there's lots to be done! We've patients to treat!" I think he was talking in a loud voice to hide his tears.

The relief team put their supplies of medicine and rice and tins of food on the porch of the cottage and went downhill, through the woods to the stream to wash off their bloodstains.

The house was full of the smell of iodine and cresol. It made us feel a little easier. Over a hundred patients from the hospital were in Koba and the valley, and how happy they would be when they saw the doctors and nurses!

When the relief team had washed off the blood and dirt they came back to the house, and only then would Kayano and Makoto go near their father. These men and women had spent three days and nights in the compound of the ruined hospital with their patients and they were near collapse. After taking some food they stretched themselves out on mats and fell sound asleep, both doctors and nurses, some of them snoring loudly.

The bodies of Shizuko and Uncle Suematsu had to be attended to, and since Sadako and Sayoko were taking care of Ritsuko it was up to Tatsue and myself to go.

All the bodies we saw were quickly decaying from the summer heat and had turned dark. With their puffed-up look they were a frightful sight. The smell was enough to stop your breath. What a pity, to have left these poor people so! We saw a great number of corpses rotting on the banks of the river and in the fields outside town, and people were walking among them, trying to find missing relatives. Dozens of flies buzzed around each corpse; whenever we passed one we would start up clouds of flies, which alighted on our backs and heads, fouling us with the stench of the corpse. This in turn attracted more flies, and they swarmed after us, their wings setting up a hum.

When we got to Urakami, Shizuko's body was all

swollen and changed in just one day. Her face had turned black and her eyes were popping. Her tongue hung out on her chin. Her nose dripped some shiny stuff. She was such a sight that we couldn't have brought ourselves to touch her had we not been blood relatives. When we took hold of her arms, sheets of decayed skin came right off. She was heavy besides, and it seemed too much for two women but a relative of ours, Sakujiro Matsuda, helped us drag her out of the shelter. We piled up some sticks and twigs and set the body afire.

If only I had burned her yesterday! She wouldn't have gotten to look like this. I wouldn't have to remember her this way. But I had been so afraid of the planes that I had simply fled and left her. There were planes today, but I was not going to run away again. Scared as I was, I gathered the wood and stayed while the body burned.

A relief team had set up an emergency sick-bay in the battered school building. We watched them moving people who had died during the night out into the yard, lining them up in rows. How could so many have died in one night?

Many of these bodies were unmarked. I heard that

people who had not been wounded and seemed to be all right would begin feeling out of sorts and all of a sudden drop dead. It made me panicky. Here I was bustling around now, but I might suddenly go off myself. All there had been was one big flash, but whatever it was it still had a terrible curse on us. I felt that if I was going to have to live in such terror, I would rather have been killed instantly.

The people cremating the corpses were doing it at the risk of their lives. With planes flying overhead all the time, the smoke made them good targets. But by evening all the bodies had been attended to. They were just piles of bones now, young and old alike. It's a lucky family that lives and dies in the natural order—first the grandfather, then the father, then the son. . . . But generations didn't count any more, in Urakami.

Tatsue and I got back to Koba after the sun had gone down. Our grief had been too much—we could no longer feel anything. A sliver of a moon came out. I went down to the stream and bathed. In the moonlight my body looked as though it had lost every ounce of fat in these last four days. I felt as though the sticky "thread of death" were wound round and round me. I picked up a handful of sand from the bed of the stream and scrubbed and scrubbed myself all over. Then I rinsed my mouth and bathed my eyes, ears, and nose. I combed my hair and felt a little fresher.

The fireflies had lived through the blast in the shelter of the valley, and they were flying around with their reflections twinkling in the stream. The breathing of the live bugs and the smell of the grass gave life to the air. It was good to take a deep breath—the delicious air filled my lungs. . . . In Urakami the air had been dead with the stench of bodies. It must be poisonous. I was sure people were going to die from it.

When I got back to the cottage they were saying prayers for the dead in a dark room. With so many dead to pray for, we would never finish saying the prayer of the rosary. . . .

Poor little Ritsuko was still sobbing, "Mama! Where's Mama?" The diarrhea had become worse—there was hardly time to get her to the toilet and Sadako and Sayoko had to stay with her constantly. They told me Dr. Nagai had examined her and said there wasn't a thing to be done.

At midnight the relief team was still out.

The fourth day after I was dull and tired all over.

I got up with my head feeling heavy and thought I was going to be dizzy. Was it the poisonous air of Urakami? . . .

The story was going around that the ruins of Urakami ran for two miles from north to south and that if you walked through them you would get diarrhea and if you tried to take care of many of the dead you would come down with some terrible disease, and sometimes you would start coughing up blood. Was this going to happen to me too? I wondered. Tatsue was complaining of a headache also.

The relief team went out again in the early-morning hours while it was still dark, because there might be air raids after the sun came up.

Mr. Tagawa, the schoolmaster, decided to take his two boys and stay with some relatives in Kikitsu. The two children were well enough, though the younger had some iodoform smeared on the crown of his head. Mr. Tagawa taught in grade school and had his work to attend to, but with his wife and home and two of his children gone, and these two little tots trailing around after him, he hadn't been able to get back on the job. He couldn't make up his mind whether to leave the children some place or to go and live in the

58

school and keep them with him. The members of our *tonarigumi* *—those who were still alive—were here at the cottage for the time being, and, what with the great crowd of patients and the relief squad bustling about, the place was in an uproar. I suppose that was why Mr. Tagawa decided to go to his relatives, even though they lived some distance away. Ever since the blast he had been so helpful, leading us and guiding us, and now that he was in a fix you would have thought we would repay him by offering to take care of the children.

But we didn't know what was going to become of us. We all thought we had a much better chance of dying than of living, so we couldn't bring ourselves to offer. In the first place, there was food to think about. There was enough of a supply for a few days, but it was sure to be gone by the end of the week. Since early in the morning Dr. Nagai had been asking around, trying to find out how he could get his hands on some rations for his rescue team, and this must have helped

* A sort of neighborhood association consisting generally of eight to ten households. During the war these units were a great convenience to the government, which transmitted directives through the *tonarigumi* chairmen. The associations saw to the distribution of ration cards, collected salvage materials, sounded air-raid alarms, ran the shelters, and so forth.

to make up Mr. Tagawa's mind for him. As he left, he said, "Well, goodbye, everybody. Thanks for all your trouble," and nobody tried to stop him. We might have said, "Don't go, please stay at least until young Naoshi's head wound is healed." But nobody said it.

We told ourselves that if we offered to take the children and the house were hit in an air raid, it would be our fault if anything happened to them. But the real reason was that it was going to be hard enough to stay alive ourselves, and impossible to worry about anyone else.

Ritsuko became weaker and weaker. She was going to die any moment. The relief squad had been out since early morning, and by late that night they had not yet returned. I don't know how many times I went outside to watch for them. At about twelve o'clock they returned, in a state of collapse. They were almost too tired to talk, but they told us that the number of patients down in the valley was tremendous. The wounds were horrible and treating them took a long time. One student had been cut in a hundred and twenty places by pieces of glass. The slivers had to be taken out one by one, and then each of the hundred and twenty wounds had to be sterilized and bandaged. I heard the story from a nurse and it made my hair stand on end. How painful even a single splinter in your finger is!

The doctors gave Ritsuko all kinds of treatment and medicine, but she was beyond hope. They told us many other children had died the same way.

On the fifth day after, on Dr. Nagai's order, Ritsuko was moved to the cellar floor. The ground floor was jampacked with people, and a patient who kept having attacks of diarrhea could not be left there. Since the toilet was on the cellar floor it was certainly more convenient to have her there. Besides, she would be the only patient, and it would be quiet for her. But the cellar floor was used as a storeroom for kindling wood and vegetables, and for a bed there was nothing but some planks laid over the kindling wood. I couldn't bear to see poor little Ritsuko put in such a place. If the doctor's own child, Kayano, had got the diarrhea he certainly wouldn't have put her there, and Ritsuko was near death. It was only because her parents were not here to watch out for her—that was why she had to lie in a storeroom with a bare floor. Should she have been treated that way just because she was an orphan? If Shizuko had been alive, even if Ritsuko were sure to die she would never have stopped giving the

61

child every care and she would have prayed and prayed and done everything she could to prolong the little thing's life for a day, even half a day. . . . But with her mother dead and her father away at war and probably dead too, if the child lived she would be an orphan. The way the doctor talked he seemed to feel that that was what Ritsuko had to look forward to. He didn't say it, but he seemed to mean that it would almost be better for her to die.

The little hands were turning icy and Sadako got down beside her and rubbed them. There were dark-red spots on Ritsuko's hands and all over her body. Dr. Nagai's medicine did no good—what treatment could do any good, with this dreadful new disease?

By evening she was hanging by a thread. Her poor little body twisted and turned. We could only stand around helpless, praying the Holy Mother to aid us.

Suddenly she writhed in agony. The convulsions almost stopped her breath. She began hawking and spitting out dark-red things. Phew! The raw stink! It was blood. Khup! Khup! She kept hawking and spitting up clumps of blood.

This stopped, and the little thing fainted.

Just before midnight Ritsuko's body became rigid—and so her spotless soul went to heaven.

We got down on the cold, bare floor around the tiny body and wept. . . . When Ritsuko's father went overseas he had told Shizuko over and over again to take good care of her, and then Shizuko had given her into my care with her dying breath that day in the air-raid shelter. And now the child was dead. Surely it was to redeem all of us that this sinless baby had suffered such agony.

At last the long night lifted. It was the Feast of the Assumption. If this had been peacetime we would have made big, puffy buns of bean jam and Ritsuko would have had a good time. But today there would be no *manju* and Ritsuko was cold and dead. Yet surely her soul had risen to the side of the Holy Mother where she must be having great happiness, greater even than the bean-jam buns could ever have given her.

We bathed her face and there was no trace of her pain. She looked like an angel.

We all went to church for the Mass of the Assumption. The chapel was filled. Those who did not enter stood outside in the shade of camellia trees, paying deep attention. The crowd was great because there were many from the Urakami parish. Had people ever before listened so hard to a mass? I thought. . . .

Suddenly there was a roar of planes passing over at a low altitude, and we had to break off. Father Shimizu raised the crucifix and we all moved to the air-raid shelter in the side of the hill back of the church. In the shelter, candles were lit and they burned with a gentle flame. Those outside offered the prayer of the rosary. The sky was full of planes.

When the planes had gone, I stopped in at the parish house to see Sami Urata. It seemed years since I had last seen her. She told me that Sojiro had met his end peacefully and nobly, consoled by the last rites. That day, five days before, when I had found Sami in the ruins, she had been well enough to hurry from Urakami with the baby in her arms; but now she and the infant were both suffering from the awful disease. They had severe diarrhea and sores in their mouths. Yellowish blisters had come out around their lips. It was the sign of the fatal disease. People were dropping dead of it one after another—even people who had suffered no wound at the time of the explosion.

I decided I wanted to have a coffin made for Ritsuko,

but there wasn't a chance. Wherever I asked they told me twenty or thirty people were dying in the valley every day, and that I would just have to cremate her in the clothes on her back. There simply wasn't any lumber and anyhow the living were far fewer than the dead. . . .

I picked up a wicker basket—the kind used by vegetable-peddlers—, wrapped the little body in a straw mat, and put it in the basket. I hung the basket from a pole and balanced it on my shoulder as I started down toward Urakami. Along the way I passed many people cremating their dead. There were no coffins. The bodies were put on piles of wood and burned. It was done like a fish fry at a picnic. Was it proper to treat a human body so? I wondered. But the invasion of the Allied forces was closing in, and the roar of the planes in the sky never stopped. After all, these people were risking their lives just by cremating the corpses. . . .

I burned Ritsuko in the yard of the Technical High School, right up the hill from the house where she had lived. On the grounds of the elementary school Hatsue Tsujimoto was being cremated by her aunt, Matsu Moriuchi. Last night, she said, Hatsue had had a mis-

65

carriage and she had died this morning at almost the same moment as her eldest boy, Isamu. Old Auntie Matsu told me that Hatsue had had the diarrhea too. Isamu and Ritsuko had been in about the same spot when the blast came, and they had died the same day and in the same way. It was enough to give one the shivers. The thing must have been some sort of death ray.

As Ritsuko's body was going up in smoke we heard unexpected news—Japan had surrendered! The war was over! . . .

The war had begun on the Feast of the Immaculate Conception, December 8th. The war had ended on the Feast of the Assumption, August 15th. How unhappy the Holy Mother must have been all this time! How she must have labored in her heart to bring peace back to the world! How many cruel swords must have pierced her pure heart!

Now suddenly this hateful war was over and the light of peace shone on the wastes. The ugly skeletons of the munitions plants showed up clearly—what madmen we were to have let these plants be set up in Urakami and to have worked in them to make money!

Four years have passed. I am now married to Sakutaro Matsumoto and have become the mother of two children.

Since having the children I can understand the feelings of a mother. How it must have torn Shizuko's heart when, with her dying breath, she entrusted Ritsuko to me! Without thinking, I had promised her, "All right, don't worry," and then I let Ritsuko die without giving her a mother's care. . . . I feel so guilty—I feel that I have failed Shizuko. . . .

This spring a postcard came unexpectedly from Ritsuko's father. He was alive in Siberia:

I have been very well ever since. Are you and Ritsuko in good shape too? How is your father and the whole family? I suppose they are all well. And has Shigeharu come home from the Nampo theater? * Just wanted to know. How is Nagasaki doing? I suppose there are a good many American soldiers there. Please tell my relatives I am all right and give them my regards. See that Ritsuko doesn't get sick or have any accidents. Goodbye.

It was addressed to Shizuko. If he came back he would find everyone dead, everyone he had been look-

* The South Pacific area.

ing forward to seeing. He had been so anxious about Ritsuko when he went away . . . when he came back, what would he say to me? And what would I be able to say to comfort him? I dread the day and still, at the same time, I am anxious to see him again.

The Shigeharu mentioned in the letter was Shizuko's younger brother, who had been on Timor Island way down in the Nampo theater. As soon as the war was over he was shipped home by the British. He said that during the voyage he had been a prisoner in name only, and had had complete liberty and plenty of good food —in fact, he said it was a splendid sightseeing trip. He now has a happy family and a cute little boy. Only the Soviet Union has failed to send back the Japanese prisoners of war, but it seems the ones in Siberia don't know that.

In the card Shizuko's husband had taken it for granted that there must be American soldiers in Nagasaki, but there is not a single one here now. There are a good many travelers from abroad. One would never believe this was Japan under a military occupation—it is such a quiet, peaceful city.

Just from what the card said it is easy to see that

68

the Japanese prisoners of war don't know the truth. Another message reached us this summer:

What a long time since we have been in touch! It's my fault. Please excuse me. Since my last message I suppose everyone at home has been in good shape. I am fine, and just like everybody in the Soviet Union I'm getting everything I need, so please don't worry. We've been through a cold winter but we are now having a warm spring—we do get them here. I suppose it is getting gradually warmer there, too. But I guess you are having a tough time, what with hunger and inflation and heavy taxes. Here in the Soviet Union prices are dropping steadily and the people are living quietly and happily. We Japanese must strive to build this sort of country and the sooner the better! That is our duty! Let's get busy and go to it! Goodbye.

When I read this I wept. Who could believe it had been written of his own free will? Was there even the slightest sign of affection from him as Shizuko's husband? The prisoners must have been lined up in a row and forced all together to write words dictated by some commissar. When he had to write that he has every-

69

thing he needs and that he is living quietly and peacefully along with the citizens of the Soviet Union, how that must have turned his stomach! Every now and then a Japanese who has done forced labor in a Soviet concentration camp comes back and tells us the real truth, which is a long way from freedom and peace. It is a horrible existence. Some of them have lost all their teeth and aged twenty years. What experiences they have had!

CHAPTER V

Tatsue Urata's Story

The narrator, Tatsue Urata, was in her early thirties at the time of the explosion. She was a mile or so from Urakami, having gone to Topposui to leave some wheat at the mill there. Being a sister of Fujie Urata Matsumoto, her relationships are the same as given in Chapter IV, and the prefatory note to that chapter should be consulted. Additional persons appearing here are:

Akiko Tsuchie (see Chapter II) and her parents.
Kikue Urata, another cousin.
Masaichi Urata, Tatsue's and Fujie's younger brother.
Akiharu Moriyama, another cousin, and his wife Tomi.

*T*he sirens howled early that morning. I carried my sick mother to the shelter picka-back. The whole *tonarigumi* used the shelter, which was well hidden from the air. Its entrance was in a fig orchard, and there was another opening through a hut eighteen yards away, part of the distance running under Dr. Nagai's house. From the entrance you went downstairs and along a corridor about ten yards to a

71

reinforced chamber, and from the chamber you could get out above ground by a trapdoor into the hut.

After a while the all-clear sounded and we all came out. If it hadn't been for the all-clear we would have stayed down in the shelter.

We all came out and sat around gossiping on the doctor's *engawa*. It was cool and pleasant, and the sky very clear, and we chattered a lot—it was the feeling of relief. My mother was actually laughing out loud. She never laughed much, she wasn't well.

It was just a lot of aimless chatter. There were a few neighbors around, but mostly we were all in the family. My cousin Midori Nagai decided it was a good day to spread some beans around in the garden to dry. Next week would be the Feast of the Assumption, and she wanted to have beans ready so she could make some of her delicious *manju* and give her children, Makoto and Kayano, a treat. (Everybody ate *manju* on the Feast of the Assumption—in fact, we even used to call it the "Feast of the Manju.") So Midori dumped out a sackful she had just picked. Midori was always good at raising beans. She'd had a very good crop this year.

How she loved those children! She was strict with

them, but the rest of us felt she was almost too indulgent when it came to things for them to eat, or their clothes, or toys and things for them to play with, and so on. Take their clothes, for example. Most of the mothers in our neighborhood made their children's clothes big and roomy. The children were growing, and that way their clothes would last two or three years. But not Midori. She made her youngsters new clothes every year. Baggy clothes, she said, interfered with their freedom of movement, and besides, clothes that didn't fit nicely were bad for their sense of beauty.

Midori taught cooking, sewing, and handicrafts at a girls' high school. She made all her family's clothes herself. She could make delicious dishes out of vegetables, and she knew how to use things that people usually waste, like calves' stomachs. With food scarce we were all using wild plants and pine needles and things like that in our cooking—we had learned how from Midori. We picked up some delicious recipes from her. Every now and then she would have the women of the neighborhood in for a demonstration. She had good ideas on how to keep children fed properly with a war going on.

We'd had so many air raids in Nagasaki that Midori

had begun to worry about the children. Bombs had fallen in our neighborhood, and sometimes machine-gun bullets from strafing planes sprayed on the roofs of our houses. She wanted to send the youngsters to the country, but they refused to leave her—they kicked up such a fuss that she had to give in and keep them with her. But two days ago we had heard about a dreadful new kind of bomb falling on Hiroshima, so Midori had taken the children to Koba and left them.

Of course, she would have preferred to stay with them, but that was against regulations. Women were not allowed to leave a house unoccupied. With the men all working during the day in offices or factories, there were only the women left to keep fires from spreading in case of an air raid. And anyway, Midori had a sense of duty toward the rest of us—she believed in "Love thy Neighbor." Besides, she was chairman of the federation of the women's societies in Urakami, and that gave her many responsibilities which kept her from leaving town.

So we were sitting around on the *engawa* and Midori was spreading the beans in the garden just a few feet away, and my mother said, "Little Kayano must be very lonely up at the cottage"; but if anybody was

lonely it was my mother. Makoto and Kayano used to
come over to our house every day. They loved to hang
around their "Granny Take" and get her to play with
them, and she always spoiled them.

My mother had no grandchildren of her own. My
sister Fujie and I were both past thirty and not married
on account of the war, and our brother Masaichi had
been overseas for goodness knows how long. So my
mother didn't have any grandchildren and she had
wanted grandchildren badly. Kayano and Makoto were
like grandchildren to her, and she missed them terribly.

My mother's remark made Midori look a little sad.
She answered, "I guess so, I suppose she must be lonely,
mustn't she? After all, there aren't any other houses
around . . . and Makoto is probably down swimming
in the river all the time, he's a regular frog, that one!
I wonder what Kayano is doing now? Probably playing
'Mummy' with her doll."

Just then Mrs. Tsuchie broke in, as though she had
had some kind of premonition, "I think maybe I'll send
Akiko to the cottage, too."

Her husband had been in the Department of Oph-
thalmology at the Medical College, but he had been
drafted and sent to an army hospital in Hiroshima. Mi-

dori said to her, "You're worrying, aren't you, Mrs. Tsuchie? I do so hope your husband is all right."

"Of course, I'm worried, I'm so worried I don't know what to do! That dreadful bomb! He must have been wounded—maybe he's even going to die! I so wish I could go to him—but you just can't get on a train."

Nobody said anything for a while. We were all thinking about Dr. Tsuchie and we were thinking: Might not this mysterious, awful new Hiroshima bomb be dropped on Nagasaki too? Then the talk started again and somebody, I don't remember who, said, "You know these leaflets the Allied planes have been dropping?:

Back in April, Nagasaki was all flowers;
August in Nagasaki, there'll be flame showers."

"Shh!" exclaimed Midori. "Don't repeat what the leaflets said—the military police will get you!"

But I said, "Well, they've always been reliable, haven't they? Whenever the leaflets said a city was going to be bombed, it was, wasn't it? At least, that's what I hear."

And somebody else said, "Yes, they have been reliable, that's what upsets the generals and the government. The people read the leaflets and the army can't do anything to stop the bombings from happening!"

"Don't talk like that! You'll be taken for a spy, ha-ha!" Everybody had a good laugh.

We kept talking about air raids and bombings for a little while, then my mother turned to Midori and asked, "How is Dr. Nagai?"

And Midori answered, "He stayed over at the college last night. You know, I think I'll make him some lunch and bring it over. I wish I had some ham in the house, how he loves ham sandwiches! I haven't been able to get any since the raids became so nasty."

My mother asked, "How is he feeling these days? Does he seem to be getting any better?"

The question made Midori look depressed again. She answered, "No, anybody who is sick and works as hard as he does can't help getting worse, even if what they had was perfectly curable at first. He's not well. I'm very worried." Then she asked us all to pray for Dr. Nagai. "Please say special prayers for him, won't you all? It's important to eat well and get plenty of rest and all that, but our prayers will help him much more, I'm sure of it."

The doctor had had leukemia for some time—he got

it working in the radiology laboratory—and lately any-body could see he was getting worse. The only thing still big about him was his stomach. His arms and legs were wasting away and his face had no flesh, the bones just stuck out. Once, lately, I had seen him going to the Medical College leaning on Midori with his arm around her shoulder. It looked almost as if she were dragging him along.

Midori never showed him her feelings; she always tried to act cheerful in front of him. But once he was out of the house and she saw him wobble along down the road she would break down and cry, like a woman.

Midori believed very strongly in the power of prayer. Lately she had started saying special prayers to the Holy Mother, and many times, with air raids going on, she had gone to offer prayers to Our Lady of Lourdes at the convent in Hongochi. I don't think the doctor ever knew about it.

So Midori asked us all to pray for him, and my mother sighed and said, "It would be nice if he could take a rest, wouldn't it, when he's as sick as all that?"

And Midori answered, "He could if it weren't for the war. The hospital's filled with air-raid casualties, and he's busy all the time, what with treating patients and teaching classes." She stared over at the hill where the buildings of the college were.

My mother tried to change the subject, but there weren't many other things to talk about. She asked about Isematsu. "Oh, I meant to ask you, speaking of casualties, is Isematsu any better?" Isematsu was Mother's cousin's son. Both his legs had been broken by bomb fragments in an air raid a week before, and he was now in the college hospital. Mother had been worrying about him.

Just then my cousin Kikue came along, looking for me to go to the mill at Topposui with her. The Allies were supposed to be getting ready for an invasion, and we were trying to stock up on flour in case of a long siege. We used to take advantage of the breathing spells between one air raid and the next to bring wheat to the mill—it took three days before it was ready. "Tatsue," she said, "let's go take some wheat to the mill," and I asked Mother if she minded.

Mother said, "All right, but please hurry back. I don't want to be alone if the planes come. Be sure to be back by lunchtime."

Kikue asked, "Do you want to come along, Cousin Midori?"

Midori thought it over for a moment, and then she answered, "I think I'll go this afternoon. Right now I'm going to carry the doctor some lunch, and after that I'll go up to Koba; I want to see how Kayano and Makoto are getting along. I'll drop some wheat at the mill on my way to Koba."

But Mrs. Tsuchie said, "I think I'll go along with you two. I want to see if I can pick up some vegetables from the farmers around there."

This was how we separated into two groups, the ones that were going to be safe and the ones that were going to be killed. Mrs. Tsuchie and Kikue and I left the doctor's house; the rest stayed there, chatting, having a good time.

Thirty minutes later the atom bomb went off in the air half a mile from the doctor's house.

Kikue and I had left the wheat to be ground in Topposui and were resting in the shade under a tree. All of a sudden, without warning, there was a terrific roar overhead. It was the kind of noise the airplanes made when they zoomed up to gain altitude after releasing their bombs, a sound as though the sky were being scooped out with a sharp tool.

I thought, Here it comes!, and dodged behind a rock. Suddenly there was a blinding flash. A great red flash of light shot up! I thought a bomb had hit right in front of me. I threw myself headlong, flat on the ground, and stayed there with my face buried in the dirt, not daring to move. Then I heard the crackle-crackle of something burning. I raised my head just enough to see. It was the thatched roofs of the farmhouses going up in flames. I realized the flash must have set them on fire. I was down in a ravine and nothing happened there, but across the top of the mountain in front of me was an enormous, horrible red cloud going up and up. I saw that it must be over Urakami.

I was worried about Mother, and got up off the ground to run home and find her. But my legs were paralyzed. The cloud thing was growing like something alive—it already blotted out most of the sky. I was so frightened that my legs would not go forward. People were running for the air-raid shelter next to the road . . . Without thinking I started running with them, and jumped into the shelter along with everybody else.

Though I was terribly worried about my mother I was unable to leave the shelter. I stood with some others in the entrance, watching the cloud. Soon we could make out black smoke going up from the other side of the mountain, under the place where the great pillar of cloud hung in the sky. All of Urakami must be afire. We looked at each other and said, "What in the world can it be!"

After about a half-hour a young fellow came staggering along from the direction of Urakami, his shirt and trousers in tatters. The skin was peeling off his face and chest and hands. He was black all over—I suppose it was dirt that had stuck to him where the skin had peeled off; his whole body was coated with it and the blood trickling from his wounds made red streaks in the black.

I called to him, "What's happened? What's happened to you!"

He seemed at first not to have heard. Then, as if waking from sleep, he turned slowly toward me. As his eyes fell on us, standing in the mouth of the shelter, his body seemed to loosen and he let himself sink to the ground. Lying there he took a deep breath and forced out an answer.

"You never saw anything like it! Urakami is all fire!"

In another minute or two more people came along. They were every one ragged and grimy and bleeding.

82

They weren't local people; in fact, most of them were complete strangers to me. I suppose somehow or other they had escaped the fire, and had taken the first road out of town, never minding where it went. They all had bad burns; not one was completely dressed—some were almost naked. We asked this one or that one what had happened, always getting the same answer: "I have no idea what happened! A tremendous flare of light and suddenly I found myself in this condition!" We gave them first aid as best we could.

Some, their teeth chattering, kept asking for water and a few of those in the shelter screwed up enough courage to run and get some from the spring in Topposui. The injured gulped it down, but it made them retch: After a pause they wanted more, yet they couldn't hold it—no sooner did they drink than they vomited it out.

The sky was dark like a sky after the sun has gone down, but terrible. We couldn't tell whether it was from the cloud or the smoke. We heard planes flying around overhead but the black stuff hid them.

All this time I hadn't set foot outside the shelter. As between myself and Mother, saving my own skin had won out. I cried to the others, "I'm going to Urakami

and find my mother," and I tried to pull myself together and go, but one of the injured people stopped
me . . . that is, I let him stop me.

He said, "Keep away from Urakami, the whole place
is flames. You'll only be risking your life and you won't
be able to do any good. There's nobody left alive."
That gave me my excuse.

After about two hours the smoke across the mountain
lightened, and Kikue and I decided to go back to Urakami. She had left her mother at home too.

We did not take the main road that ran along the
river, because that would have taken us straight into
town, and with so many houses on fire we knew we
wouldn't be able to get through to our own neighborhood. We took instead the road across the mountain
that started from Mikumigochi and climbed up to
Sandama-*toge* * and then dropped down to Motohara.
That was only a quarter of a mile from where we lived,
and from there we thought we would be able to cut
through the fields near the base of the mountain and
get near our homes.

We started climbing. Just before we got to the ridge

* The suffix -*toge* indicates a mountain pass.

84

we came upon a young woman lying in the road with two children. She had fearful burns all over her neck and chest. We went over to her. We couldn't tell whether we knew her or not. Her face was one blister, swollen, with the skin starting to come off. She had no hair—it was singed off to the roots. She couldn't see, but she heard us coming, and she said something in a faint voice, something we could hardly hear . . . "Please, take the babies with you!" She was holding on to them as though they might run away, although they were in as bad a state as she was. They couldn't even cry—all they could do was make gasping sounds in their throats. The three of them were barely breathing, and Kikue and I saw they were going to die; it was simply a question of whether the babies or the woman would die first. She knew she hadn't long, and I guess she could hear the planes overhead. That must have been why she wanted us to take them along.

We stood there a moment not knowing what to do. Then she asked us for water, and as I remembered passing a pond a little way downhill I went back to get her some. The first time we passed the pond I hadn't noticed the oily film on its surface or how the grass and the leaves on the trees around were shiny-wet. I touched some leaves; they felt oily. There must have been a rain of oil.

I fetched water for the woman and her children, but we didn't want to stay around and watch them retching —we knew they would throw it right up again. We gave them the water and left quickly.

When we got to Sandama-*toge* there was a hot wind rolling up the mountainside that made me so dizzy I thought I was going to faint. Down below us was Urakami flaming—one look and I changed my mind, I knew it was hopeless trying to find Mother there. All I could make out was the three-story red-brick Sei Furanshisuko * Hospital. Flames were shooting from its windows.

The hills around the Urakami basin were bald, their greenery gone. The tree trunks had been broken off a few feet from the ground; here and there the upper part of a tree still hung from its stump, the top branches resting on the ground. I could see that the broken-off parts all pointed away from one spot—Matsuyama-*cho* —just like the spokes of a wheel, and I knew that must have been where the blast had come from.

* St. Francis.

A little farther downhill we saw a group of about thirty women and children behind some rocks. We picked our way down, and found them all saying the prayer of the rosary together. The women were sisters from the Urakami Orphanage, most of them stretched out on the ground with bad wounds. The younger nuns had burns all over their bodies, and they were half-naked. They said the flash had caught them working on the orphanage farm and scorched them instantly, clothes and skin; then the blast that followed directly after had blown pieces of skin and clothing right off their bodies.

There were some older nuns, the only ones who could still get about. They told me they had been indoors because they didn't generally do any of the farm work, and thus hadn't been hurt so badly. They were going around giving the others first aid and taking care of the children.

We left them and went down as far as the hospital. The open lot in front of the building was full of casualties, and they were still bringing them in and placing them in rows on the ground. I recognized Dr. Akizuki giving first aid, with brothers and nurses helping him.

The statue of the Archangel Michael that used to

stand in the garden was gone, blown away without a trace. We wondered, how could it be that the Great Flash was stronger even than the Archangel Michael?

I suppose if Kikue and I hadn't been together we might have been braver. Maybe we would have tried to get through the fire to our houses somehow. But being together, everything we did, every step we took, we had to talk over first, and I guess that made it harder for both of us instead of easier—to get up courage, I mean. Talking it over got us more afraid instead of less.

So we stood there on the side of the mountain gazing down at the thick smoke and the flames and we just gave up.

We turned to the left and took the road that headed east around the skirt of Mount Kompira. We kept coming upon injured people lying in the road. They had simply dropped along the way wherever their strength gave out. Some had burns on their faces so bad they couldn't see yet they could hear our footsteps and they kept calling out, "Water! Water!" There were so many of them!

We saw many dead, too. Every woman we saw I

spoke to, lest she be my mother; some of them nobody could have recognized. But I did not find my mother, nor did I see a single person from my whole neighborhood. I felt crushed—if I hadn't found her by now there was no hope, I knew. Overhead we could hear the planes coming and going and coming and going.

We fell in with some people following the road into Nishiyama-*cho,* in the valley east of Mount Kompira, away from the fires. There we stayed overnight with friends. They told us that a lot of stuff like ashes and bits of paper had come down shortly after the explosion. They said a west wind must have picked it up from Urakami and blown it eastward over Mount Kompira and dumped it on Nishiyama. I found out that here, too, had come the same kind of black, oily rain that fell at Sandama.

Next morning I heard that the fires were all out in Urakami, so I started over. I took the road across Mount Kompira and stopped at Isematsu's house in Teraida, to find out whether they had heard from him since the explosion; but they hadn't, or from his wife Yuki, either. She'd been staying at the college hospital nursing him. *

* Especially during the war, because of the shortage of nurses, relatives of hospital patients were frequently called upon to take care of them.

Isematsu's sister, Taki, had gone looking for them although she was in a bad state herself—she'd been so concerned about her brother they couldn't keep her from going. When I heard this it pricked me like a needle.

My cousin Akiharu Moriyama's wife, Tomi, was there too, with her two little daughters. Akiharu had sent her there to get her out of Urakami—their next baby was due any day and Urakami was no place for her, with air raids going on all the time. She said she'd been feeling pains since the explosion; they were like labor pains, but not exactly the same either. She was worrying about Akiharu, and she wanted to come along with me, but we made her stay in bed.

Urakami was no more than a heap of ashes. Those leaflets had certainly come true.

I found where my house had been from the position of the well where we got our water.

And my mother?

In the white ashes there was one black spot, a heap of charred bones.

That was Mother!

My father had died when she was still young, and

she'd taken to selling vegetables for a living. She had supported us three by her own toil, and brought us up herself without a husband to help her. Sixty-seven years she'd lived. What an end to such a life!

Her laughter of yesterday rang in my ears as I stood there staring at the bones. I shall never forget it.

I suppose that after we left for the mill, Midori had helped her back to our house. There she had probably gone right to bed. I wonder if she saw the flash, or did the house cave in on her before she knew what had happened? Our thatched roof must have caught fire immediately.

Surely she called my name with her last breath.

And where was I? Hiding in the shelter at Topposui.

There were fresh footprints in the ashes which must be my sister Fujie's. I knew Fujie must be safe, because she had gone to Koba to work the millet patch. I decided I would find her—she was probably looking for me right now—and together we would bury Mother.

In the place that once was Mrs. Tsuchie's house, on the other side of the well, I found some small bones. These must have been her little girl's. Because there weren't any larger ones I knew Mrs. Tsuchie could not have got home before the flash.

Next to Dr. Nagai's the fig trees had been blown out of the orchard, roots and all, and without the surrounding trees the entrance to the shelter looked like the wide-open mouth of a crazy person laughing. There wasn't anyone inside. In the ashes above the shelter I found some charred bones just where Midori's kitchen had been. Yesterday she'd said no, she couldn't come along to the mill with us, she was going to make some lunch for Dr. Nagai and then she was going to see Kayano and Makoto at the cottage . . . she must have died right in the midst of making something they all liked.

There was a frying pan lying next to the bones, mashed flat.

I found my sister Fujie in Koba at the cottage. Besides Fujie there were Sadako, Sayoko, Takeo, Ritsuko, Makoto, and Kayano. When Fujie told me about Shizuko, how worried she'd been over little Ritsuko when she was only minutes away from death, I thought of my mother and of how I had stayed in hiding in the shelter, taking care only of myself. It felt as though a nail had been driven into my heart.

Next morning Fujie and I went back to Urakami and gathered up Mother's bones and buried her in Akagi Cemetery.

About Mrs. Tsuchie. Later on I found out what had happened to her. After she'd left us at Topposui she'd gone on to Mikumigochi to buy vegetables, and she was there when the flash came. Since she'd left her little girl home alone she hurried back to Urakami by the same path Kikue and I took a couple of hours later. Of course, the whole town was blazing, but that hadn't stopped her. She had wriggled and squirmed through the smoke and the flames until she got to her house. There she began screaming, "Akiko! Akiko!," and finally, becoming frantic, she had rushed around the neighborhood half-crazy, trying to find the child, until she was overcome by the smoke and collapsed. She had suffered horrible burns; both her legs had been scorched black. Someone had found her lying there and managed to get her aboard a train and send her to a hospital. She's all right now, I understand; she's living in Matsue,* where her husband, Dr. Tsuchie, was born. Dr. Tsuchie died at Hiroshima.

When I heard Mrs. Tsuchie's story it made me think of poor Eiko. She was an orphan who had been brought up by a relative of mine. This woman had one child of her own, a girl older than Eiko. She had not been in Urakami when the bomb fell; she'd been up to the mountains for some reason. When she saw the flash she became anxious about her daughter, and hurried down toward Urakami. Somewhere along the way she heard somebody calling her, "Mother! Mother!," and she turned around to find Eiko, naked and shaking, lying in the mouth of an air-raid shelter next to the road. She had hideous burns.

The old lady could see Eiko was going to die; yet she was in a pitiful state, she was suffering terribly, and at least the old lady could have made her more comfortable. But Eiko looked so horrible that the old lady could not bear to see her; she actually wanted to get away. Eiko didn't notice, she was so overjoyed to see her adopted mother. She begged the old lady to

* A town on the Sea of Japan where the author came from. Lafcadio Hearn also lived in Matsue.

cover her up, for she was cold. She said, "Mother! I couldn't go any farther. I wanted to come to you. Cover me up, I'm cold."

The old lady was wearing two layers of air-raid clothing. She could have taken one off and given it to Eiko, but she was thinking of her own daughter— maybe *she*'d need it—so she said, "Wait a minute, I'll find something. Just wait a minute, hold on to yourself . . ."; then she left Eiko and ran away.

The reason why she adopted Eiko was because she had only one child of her own, and she thought that if her daughter died before she did that would leave no one to look after her in her old age. Well, the old lady finally found her own child, a little pile of bones. And still she didn't go back to Eiko—Eiko had looked so horrible.

Eiko died the next day and some people around there buried her.

I found this out from the old woman herself. She was telling me the story of what had happened before she finally found her daughter, and she let it slip out without meaning to. That was just a few days after it happened. Nowadays, whenever she talks about it she fixes up the part about Eiko. Many times she's asked me to go and visit Eiko's grave for her. I always say, "Why don't you go yourself?," and she says, "Oh, it's such a long way, it's too far for me, I'm not so young any more. . . ." My guess is she doesn't have the nerve to stand in front of Eiko's grave.

Lately she's suddenly started acting crazy without any warning; sometimes she runs after little children and tries to catch them. I'm sure it's because they remind her of Eiko.

She keeps trying to make friends with me. I'm related to her and she's getting on in years, her heart isn't strong any more, she doesn't have either her own daughter or Eiko. But I'm not to be taken in—she's acting so nice to me now, but I know perfectly well if such a thing ever happened again she would desert me the way she did Eiko. So on the surface I act respectfully toward her, but I really despise her, I hate her!

Yet who am I to despise her when I neglected my own mother? I despise myself! I hate myself!

In the fall we built a little cabin about twelve feet square, with a galvanized iron roof, on Mrs. Tsuchie's land and nine of us set up house in it. There were Dr. Nagai and his two youngsters, Kikue and her family, and my sister Fujie and myself. We planted some wheat and raised a little spinach and a few other vegetables, and we got started building ourselves new houses where the old ones had been. By the end of autumn Fujie and I had the framework set up for ours and we prepared for a celebration. Then, the night before, my brother Masaichi suddenly turned up alive.

I was in the little cabin when I heard him outside, calling, "Mother! Mother!" I recognized his voice immediately. Fujie and I went out and there he was, stumbling around outside the new house in the dark. He was all confused—his neighborhood was in ruins and there was just a bare wooden frame where his house had been. His voice felt like a knife in a healing wound.

Why hadn't I sent Mother to Koba? She'd be alive if I had. I'd taken care to leave five or six garments in Koba so I'd have some clothes in case our house burned down in a raid. And what had I done but left my mother in Urakami?

I suppose we'd lost hope of seeing Masaichi again. I guess he himself must often have wondered whether he'd ever get home. But he never stopped trying, he so wanted to see his mother once more. I knew how much he loved her and I knew how Mother missed him and how she'd been hoping and hoping for him to come home—why hadn't I sent her to Koba with Kayano and Makoto, instead of letting her stay in Urakami to be burned alive!

We came over to him. My brother lit a match and saw only Fujie and myself; besides us, there was nothing but empty darkness. He moaned and dropped the match. There was a little red glow on the dark ground that lasted a few seconds. The three of us stood there weeping. The sound seemed to accuse me, it seemed to be saying, "You killed your mother!" I was trembling. This was the spot where Mother's bones had been.

We took Masaichi over to the hut. He pulled a little paper package from his pocket and unwrapped it. There were five lumps of sugar in it, the kind American soldiers get for breakfast, and he said, "I brought these back for Mother. I was going to give them to her as soon as I got home." He remembered Mother loved sweets and he'd saved the sugar from his breakfasts while he was being shipped home. He had several fingers missing—we noticed it as he was opening the package, he was so awkward.

He broke the lumps in half and offered us each a

piece, but I didn't care about the sugar. I just stared at his hand with the fingers missing. It made me think what a terrible war he had been in. I guess the others felt the same way. Little Makoto and Kayano came and took some sugar and licked it. Brother smiled as he watched them licking and licking; that was his first smile. It seemed he relaxed a little. He said, "My! How Makoto and Kayano have grown!"

CHAPTER VI

Matsu Moriuchi's Story

The narrator is Matsu Moriuchi, a woman of fifty-nine, single, living with her niece Hatsue, the latter's husband Mataichi Tsujimoto, and their children—two boys, Isamu and Fujio, and a girl, Kimiyo—most of whom were first introduced in Chapter IV. The other relationships mentioned in this chapter are by now familiar from earlier pages. "Auntie Matsu" survived the explosion without serious injuries, having reached the shelter at the Yamazato Elementary School in time.

*W*hen the atom bomb went off I was in an air-raid shelter, the one in the corner of the yard of the Yamazato Grade School. That was only half a mile from the spot over which the bomb exploded, but I came through although many people in the shelter and almost everybody outside it was killed or died soon after. I have no idea why I should have been spared.

I am single and I was living at that time with my niece, Hatsue Tsujimoto, and her family—her husband, Mataichi, and their three children, Isamu, Fujio, and Kimiyo. We ran a little shop, our customers being the neighborhood housewives and their children. We sold salt, *sake*,* vegetables, needles and thread, candles, toys, candy—it wasn't a hard life; we were comfortable. Mataichi was a skilled well-digger and had done many jobs in the neighborhood—in fact, the last well he dug had been for Dr. Nagai.

Isamu was eight years old, a very quiet child. He was in the second grade, and got good marks. Fujio, who was five, went to the kindergarten run by the sisters of the Society of the Infant Jesus. Fujio was a noisy, rough little rascal, not like his brother at all. He insisted on winning, whether it was games with other children or the fights he got into, or whatever. Kimiyo was a cute little thing, just two years old, and she always called me Granny, Granny, Granny. I was fifty-nine at the time.

I used to help out with the store, and every morning I went to church to hear mass; there was nothing I liked better. Mataichi and Hatsue were religious too —we got along very well together.

That morning the air-raid alarm had sounded rather early and Mataichi had gone out to patrol his beat, since he was an air-raid warden, and I myself had taken

* Japanese rice wine.

the three children to the shelter in the schoolyard, about a hundred yards away. That left Hatsue to stay home and watch the house.

There wasn't any raid, though. At ten o'clock we heard the all-clear, and since none of us ever liked to stay in the shelter any longer than necessary, it was so dark and damp, we all breathed a sigh of relief and came right out. Most of the people went back home or to work. The children ran to the sandpile and the swings in the playground, and some of the school-teachers went back to digging a new shelter near the first. They had very good teamwork—the one who was acting as foreman kept counting "One! Two! Three! Four!" to keep them in rhythm. It was a beautiful day altogether; there were big clouds all around but over the harbor there wasn't a speck in the sky. The bright sunlight made a peaceful scene. We were glad to have been spared a raid.

Myself, I was wondering whether to let the children play or to take them right home, so I sent Isamu back to find out what Hatsue wanted me to do. He came back in a few minutes and said, "Mother says she's getting lunch and she'll call us as soon as it's ready, and she says we'd better stay in the shelter because the radio said there were two big planes over Shimabara heading west."

When I heard that, it made me uneasy. One of the teachers digging the new shelter asked, "What's that? Big planes? They must be B-29's. I wonder what they're up to? . . . Shimabara, is it? That means Unzen-*dake*,* and if they're coming westward they must be going to hit Nagasaki. They ought be here by now."

No sooner had he said it than we heard the engines above us.

"Here they come!" the teacher shouted. I called to the children, "Hurry! All inside!"

Fujio, who was a quick little fellow, jumped right into the shelter, while I picked up little Kimiyo and carried her. Isamu stayed behind to call the other children—he was really a fine boy—, and then came in himself.

I was about three yards inside the shelter and had turned around to see if Isamu was behind me. At that instant there was a blinding light.

It was a brilliant blue flare. In my whole life I'd never seen anything so brilliant. Just before it came one of

* -*dake*—"mountain."

the teachers had been measuring something at the entrance to the shelter. He was stripped to the waist and had the tape stretched out, holding one end in each hand. The brilliant light made him look like a beautiful piece of sculpture.

That's all I can remember. I have no idea how long it was before I came to. I found myself lying in a funny position, and the first thing I was conscious of was that my whole body ached, especially between my backbone and my left shoulder. I couldn't move my left arm at all. My head pained. I must have been hurled against the wall by the blast, and knocked out.

Somehow our own three children had escaped without a scratch. They were sitting on the floor around me, trembling like leaves; I tried to get up to see what was making them tremble, and found I had no control over my limbs. But I managed to turn my head enough to see outside the shelter— Oh! What a sight!

In the dim light coming through the mouth of the shelter I saw a huddle of half-naked people strewn about the entranceway. Their bodies were puffed up like balloons, their skin was peeling off in strips— hanging down like the shreds of a rag. They were so still I thought they were dead, but they weren't; they kept moaning, "Water—give me water!" These bodies were the teachers who just a little while ago had been having such a good time digging the new shelter.

What in heaven could have happened? What could have happened to Mataichi? And Hatsue?

I told Isamu, "Go home and get Mama!," but the child wouldn't go; he said, "You can't go outside!"

"Why not?"

"The playground is all over dead people, Granny! And around our house everything is on fire!"

The child began to weep. He cried, "The school's burning too! And Daddy isn't there, I can't see him!" The air-raid wardens' headquarters was in the school building.

I tried to comfort him. I said, "Come now, no crying, no crying. Daddy and Mummy'll put out the fire and come right over and get us. . . ." But I was struggling to keep from weeping myself. I began calling, "Mataichi! . . . Hatsue! . . . Mataichi! . . . Hatsue! . . ." I was trying to get hold of myself by calling in a loud voice.

Some time passed. Then we heard Hatsue's voice outside, crying, "Isamu! Isamu! Are you there? . . . Fujio! Kimiyo!" Isamu answered from inside the shelter, "Mama!," and Fujio called out, "Here I am!" She heard their voices and came over. I saw immediately that she was limping. The whole entrance was blocked with those moaning teachers lying there and she could hardly find room to pass; she had to step over several prostrate bodies. She said "Sorry" as she did so. She had a hard time getting by—she had no more than grazed one or two of them, yet they cried out in pain.

"Where is Mataichi?"

"Where is Mataichi?"

Hatsue and I were stunned to hear each other asking the same question. Where was Mataichi!

She took Kimiyo into her arms. The little thing was the only happy one in the shelter, for she didn't know what was going on. She kept saying, "Mama, water! I want water!" Hatsue hadn't brought any water so she started to give her breast to the child. She was six months' pregnant at the time. This seemed to content little Kimiyo, but suddenly the child did a funny thing. It was almost noon and she should have been hungry, but for some reason she put the nipple right out of her mouth.

Hatsue had been in the kitchen boiling pumpkins and potatoes, and had just taken the pots off the stove

106

when there came that sudden flash and the house caved in. She was knocked to the floor alongside the sink—luckily enough, for the sink was concrete and that saved her from being crushed when one of the rafters fell. It ended up with one end on the floor and the other leaning against the sink, and herself underneath. But another beam had pinned one of her legs, and though she kept calling for help no one came. There wasn't a sound outside; that had made her all the more frightened. Finally she managed to get her leg free, and tore her way through the straw thatching of the roof to get outside.

Not a moment too soon; a minute more and she would have been burnt to a cinder along with the house. All around, everything was ablaze, and our house was about to catch fire. There hadn't been time to save a thing from the house—she'd have been swallowed up by the blaze if she'd waited for a second. So she hurried toward the shelter, but with her injured leg she hadn't been able to go very fast, and besides, the road was all in flames. She had had to pick her way through the fields from one open spot to the next, squirming through narrow spaces with the flames reaching out for her.

But what about the rest of *tonarigumi*? I asked her, what about Dr. Nagai's wife, Midori? and Keiko Moriyama? and Mrs. Tagawa? and Hatsuko Fukabori?; and what about Moshiro Moriuchi? and Mitsuyoshi Urata and Sami Urata? and Reiko's mother? and old Mrs. Take Urata? . . . I asked her about all of them but she said she didn't know, she hadn't seen them, she supposed they were dead.

I just couldn't believe it; I said, "What! Is the whole *tonarigumi* gone?" And Hatsue answered, "Not just the *tonarigumi*, the whole town."

We waited and waited and nobody came. Dr. Nagai was supposed to come if anything like this ever happened, he was supposed to bring medicine and take care of anybody who had been hurt; but he didn't come, so we knew the Medical College must have been destroyed too.

The teachers who had been working on the new shelter had all been hurt except one, who had been down inside the tunnel they were digging. He kept going to fetch water for the rest of us. Evening came on, and it was so quiet outside that I thought everybody, the whole population of Urakami, must be dead except us

108

in the shelter. It was quiet, except when one of the teachers moaned, "I'm cold! Cover me up!"

I told the beads of my rosary, which I still had on my wrist. I prayed for the living and the dead both.

During the night, all of a sudden, Hatsue began to scream. "What's the matter with Kimiyo! Oh, Kimiyo, Kimiyo! Look at her!" she cried.

I turned my head and saw that the child was having violent convulsions. She'd been quite all right up to now. Three times the convulsions seized her, and the third time she died. It was so quick it was quicker than it takes to tell. There wasn't even time to pray for help to the protectress St. Elizabeth.* Imagine! To have died so suddenly from this one flash, twelve hours later and without a mark on her!

Hatsue held the cold dead body tight in her arms; she wouldn't put it down. Then suddenly, she had no strength left. She just sank down on the floor and said nothing. The way she sat there scared me.

Some of the people in the shelter died during the night, but no one was in condition to move the bodies.

* Both Matsu and Kimiyo had been named "Erizabeto," after this saint.

Next day the first person to come along was Mr. Hatsuji Tagawa, the schoolmaster. He was the first person we saw, his was the first voice we heard. He was all right, but not his three boys in the opposite corner of the shelter from me. One of them, Toshibumi, died the very instant Mr. Tagawa walked into the shelter. He cremated Toshibumi, and Kimiyo too. It made me feel a little relieved, in spite of my grief.

He said he hadn't been able to find his wife or his two daughters; he thought they must have been burned alive in his house.

Mr. Tagawa knew all the injured teachers, for he'd taught in the Yamazato school. He got some white salve somewhere and put it on their burns, and he also got us food and gruel for those who were too sick to eat, and tea as well—goodness knows where he got it all. Then he told us what he'd just found out: it was an atom bomb.

An "atom bomb"? Whatever was that? Mr. Tagawa said it was something new that had just been invented in America.

Later, some of the teachers' relatives turned up and took them away. Mr. Tagawa started with his two remaining boys to Dr. Nagai's mountain cottage. He told us nobody knew where Dr. Nagai was. The worst thing right now was not having a doctor around; the pain in my shoulder was getting worse and Hatsue was getting weaker all the time, and Mataichi still had not come.

Little Masanori Fukabori was all alone in the shelter —I mean, none of his family were here with him. He was only seven and he kept crying, "Mama! Come and get me! . . . . Sister! Please come! . . ."

But I knew they must be dead.

Evening came. Continually Hatsue and Isamu kept wanting water.

In the morning I felt a little better, well enough to get on my feet. A man who came for one of the teachers told us that Mr. Konishi's house, straight up the hill, hadn't been burned; it had only caved in, and so I thought it might be a good idea to go up there and try and find a teapot and a few teacups. I had a hard time climbing the hill but I made it. There was a man named Takahashi at the house—I knew him by sight but not to speak to, and I started to ask him if there were any pots or cups that hadn't been smashed. But he didn't even let me finish, he just put up his hand and said, "Not a chance. I'm supposed to keep an eye on the house,

111

they asked me to." So there was nothing for me to do but leave. I said, "Oh? Is that so? Sorry to have bothered you," and I went back down the hill again.

Well, I thought, it certainly looked as though he were keeping an eye on the house. He had been clambering around the ruins as if trying to see what could be salvaged. But I thought he had jumped a little when I arrived. Why should that have been? Mr. Konishi had been killed at the factory where he worked, I knew that, and I knew besides that his wife had been pinned under the house and killed, and I knew their boy was supposed to be away. So who could have asked Takahashi to keep an eye on Mr. Konishi's house? . . .

But suddenly I felt that wasn't right, it wasn't right to be suspicious, and I was ashamed. He'd rubbed me the wrong way in not letting me borrow the teacups and straightaway I had gone and gotten suspicious of him. By the time I was a short way down the hill my conscience had begun to hurt me for having doubted Mr. Takahashi.

On the way down I heard someone calling my name. It was a Mr. Fujita, whom we had never known very well. He came over and asked about my family, being very kind and sincere. It seemed his own family had

112

all been killed. Mr. Fujita himself had lost his fingers in the war, and I guess that having known so much suffering was what made him so kind and sympathetic toward others in their troubles. I told him about Mr. Takahashi and the teacups, and he said, "Don't worry. Go on back to the shelter, the children must want you, and I'll bring some tea over later on." He was so kind that it made me cry.

Soon he brought a big kettle of tea over from his own shelter, and a supply of *nigirimeshi*.* He came back a little later with a *tatami* for the floor—ah! it was so good to have the *tatami* instead of the bare floor! I repeat, we had never known Mr. Fujita very well, we'd had barely a nodding acquaintance with him; but this was only the first of many kindnesses and favors he did us.

Hatsue and Isamu had both begun to have diarrhea, and it got steadily worse. Isamu and Fujio kept looking around the playground for pieces of paper to clean the floor with, but the attacks continued, so bad the children couldn't find enough paper. Isamu wanted to make his mother comfortable, and he was continually going

* Boiled rice compressed into balls about fist-size so that it can be eaten without utensils—a common emergency ration.

113

outside for paper or to get water from Mr. Fujita's shelter. It made him weaker to keep running around, but he paid no attention to his own comfort. If only I had been able I wouldn't have let the little fellow do everything. Watching him made me feel even worse about it.

Little Fujio was feeling fine, but he missed his father and stayed outside looking for him most of the time. After all, he was only five, and couldn't have been expected to remain with his mother every minute. In the course of an hour he would poke his head in the mouth of the shelter four or five times to ask whether Mataichi had come back. He'd say, "Is Daddy there yet?"; and all I could answer was, "No, he isn't here yet, I guess he went to town to buy us all some bedding so we'll be comfortable. Be a good boy now, he'll be along soon."

But the child wouldn't stay put. He'd say, "I'm going to find Daddy," and disappear again. Soon he would be back, exhausted and disappointed, to tell us, "I can't find him, there's nobody there." Then he would sit down in the entrance without a word, but after a few minutes he would ask, "Brother, shall we play hide-and-seek?" Poor Isamu, so weak from the diarrhea, could only answer, "No, I don't want to play today"; and the little one would say, "Aw, gee! . . . I think I'll go see the place where Kimiyo is," and run over to Kimiyo's grave. There wasn't anything there. Kimiyo's grave was just a plain mound of earth. Nobody had even put flowers on it, and if the child was looking for dragonflies I'm sure he didn't find any. In a few minutes he would be back again, asking for his Daddy.

How Hatsue must have felt, hearing all this! What it must have done to her!

As we were seeking comfort in prayer from the pain of our flesh the third night came. All day we had heard nothing but death, either this man had died or that woman had died, that was all we heard.

In the darkness I could see small fires glowing all over town, the fires of corpses being cremated.

The next day a relief team of doctors and nurses finally appeared at the school grounds and examined us. For the first time I got a close look at my own body, and saw that around my left shoulder I was all black and blue. The doctor said, "My, you must have been thrown hard!" He told me there weren't any bones broken, so that was something at least. They gave me some boracic-acid powder to make a cold compress with, saying it would soothe the pain some—but what was the good? I didn't have any basin to dissolve it in, or any towels, or enough water either.

They sat Isamu on a chair until they could get around to examining him, but he didn't have the strength to sit up; he just rolled off the chair and sprawled on the floor. One of the nurses propped him up and he slumped to the floor again, he was so weak. How could he be so weak just from an attack of diarrhea?, I wondered. The doctor who finally looked at him shook his head; he couldn't understand it. He said, "I've never seen anything like this. It's queer. It gives you a funny feeling."

As soon as the news got around that there was a relief squad at the school the casualties began appearing, most of them on stretchers. I was amazed at the number of them; where could they all have come from?, I wondered. It turned out they'd come from the various air-raid shelters in the neighborhood. A good many of those on stretchers were dead by the time they got to the school gate. Others lived long enough to have some attention, and even seemed to be feeling a little better for a moment; then suddenly died. Nearly all had their skin peeling off and their bodies swollen and blistered, and their expressions were so changed I couldn't tell whether I knew them—but I spoke to some and, sure enough, they were people I knew. Suddenly it flashed upon me that Mataichi might be among them. I looked at one after another closely, but no. There were others besides myself on the same errand.

There was no use staying at the school, so we went back to the shelter. Hatsue and Isamu were worse— going over to the relief squad had been bad for them, and they were suffering. I made them drink some medicine but it didn't help. I was still in pain myself, and still holding the useless boracic-acid powder.

People looking for their families kept coming into the shelter. They would strike a match, go to where Hatsue and Isamu and the other sick or injured were lying, study their faces closely, then say, "No, he's not here, she's not here, it's somebody else . . . ," and walk out. This upset me a great deal. What kind of people were these?, I thought. Didn't they have any consideration for strangers? Did they care only about their own families? Did they have to go around and stick their noses right into the faces of people in agony, without so much as a by-your-leave? Did they have to say in

117

such a cold way, "No, it's somebody else," and walk off without offering even a word of comfort? They simply walked around inspecting sick people and dead people without batting an eye, never shedding a tear or heaving a sigh over them.

Then it came to me suddenly that I had done exactly the same thing myself, looking for Mataichi at the school. The idea of "Love thy neighbor as thyself," that I always believed in, had just disappeared some place. I guess it was too much for any of us.

I was in such a state that I had ceased to be a human being, like a spring that gets stretched too far. When I think back on it, I think, weren't we like animals after a forest fire, hiding scared half to death, two in this hole and three in that? We did wicked things like wolves and foxes to stay alive, and even those who had always been gentle people began doing petty little bits of evil. In a crisis like this God will just have to overlook petty sins—that was the way we felt.

This new thing, this atom bomb, one thing it did was to make us unashamed of doing wrong, mean things. Hatsue's *mompe* were soiled, and I went outside to wash them. There was a spot nearby where I remembered Mataichi had dug a well, but I found the *tsurube* * gone, so there was no way to get water out of it. I went to see if any of the wells at the other houses in the neighborhood were working, but the *tsurube* were all gone. So finally I went up to the Konishi house, where I had seen Takahashi using the well. There I found his daughter washing clothes.

She was humming some tune while she scrubbed. When I came over she gave me a polite smile and congratulated me on being alive. She herself had been away in the country when the bomb fell and she was in an awfully good mood.

Well, my right arm pained me when I moved it and my left arm was completely stiff, so I thought I'd ask her to draw a bucketful when she finished her washing. I sat down and rested while she scrubbed. She was feeling so pleased with herself she said, "Well, Grandma Moriuchi, God must love both of us, mustn't he? I'd never thought I was such an especially good person but I guess I must be, after all, for it was only by God's special grace that I wasn't killed. I'm so happy that God wanted to spare me! Those people who were burned to death, they must have made God angry,

---

* Two buckets hanging on either end of a rope which passes through a pulley.

mustn't they? They must have provoked him to wrath. You must be a good person too, Grandma. You've just been hurt a little." Thus she prattled on, washing one garment after another, wringing them out and spreading them out to dry. They were beautiful one-piece flower prints, blue and yellow.

It seems to me that if the Takahashi girl had been so good and kind she would have offered to wash the *mompe* for me, but she didn't. She'd seen my stiff arm and she must have known how hard it would be for me, but as soon as she finished her own washing she glanced at the *mompe* in my hand and said, "Well, I've got to go get my rations, so I'd better hurry. Good-bye, Grandma."

It was so quick, she took me by surprise. I tried to stop her before she could get away, and asked, "I wonder if you'd do me a favor and draw some water for me before you go. I can't with my arm in this condition."

She seemed a little annoyed. "Oh, really?," she said. "Well, I'm in an awful hurry . . . but . . . oh, well, all right." So she drew some water for me, and I thanked her, and she said, "Oh, that's all right"; then she just went off and left me.

How could I do my washing when my left arm was completely stiff and I could move my right arm only with pain? I was so upset I couldn't help crying. I stood there trying to wash the *mompe* with one hand. You could hardly call it washing; all I really did was get them wet, and I couldn't wring them out with one hand. I managed to hug them with my good arm against my chest and walked back to the shelter that way, letting them drip. They were heavy, soaked. Back in the shelter I had little Fujio help me wring them out.

The chairman of our *tonarigumi* was Mr. Fukitani. Everybody thought he must have died, but a little while after I brought back Hatsue's *mompe* he came along with some food and medicine and things like that. He was always such a kind gentleman and it was so good to see him alive and well. He explained that he simply hadn't had time to come over from the City Hall, where he worked; there'd been so much to do right there. He told us his wife was dead. I remembered how Mrs. Fukitani used to run around the *tonarigumi* warning us of air raids. She would carry an empty bucket which she'd keep striking with a bamboo stick, shouting, "Everybody in the shelter! Everybody in the shelter!"

Mr. Fukitani said, "Wasn't it awful, Grandma Moriu-chi! I'm so sorry to hear Mataichi is still missing. My wife is dead."

He went on, "I want to thank you, you were always so nice to her. I found her on the path between my house and Mr. Tanaka's. I knew it was she even though the body wasn't recognizable—she was charred black! . . ." He stopped a moment to get hold of him-self. It was hard to tell such a story. Then he said, "I was going to gather up the remains when Mr. Tanaka came along. He was sure it must be *his* wife, for the body was lying about halfway between our houses. . . .

"I guess you couldn't blame him, it *might* have been his wife. Anyway, we had a quarrel about it. There really wasn't any way to tell who it was. The clothing was burned off and her ring was melted. You remember, don't you, that Mrs. Tanaka was kind of fat, but there was hardly any flesh on the bones, so we couldn't tell that way. We had quite an argument about it. Some-how I knew it was my wife. I wouldn't have argued with him over anything less important, but after all it was my *own wife;* I couldn't let him take the remains away. . . .

"Anyway, he found his wife's body later on in the

shelter under the school. She still had all her clothes. It was certainly a relief to me. This kind of thing has been going on all over. I'm willing to bet lots of people have been burying strangers in their family plots without knowing it."

One of our neighbors, Mr. Sato, had been blown right into the little air-raid reservoir behind our house. Fujio told me about it. It seems the body was still floating in the pool; the child said it was puffed up like a rubber balloon. It must have been in the water three days, this being the fourth, and nobody had fetched it out yet.

The child would see it every day and come back and tell us about it. What a dreadful thing—here was this five-year-old able to look at the dead body of one of our neighbors without being the least bit upset. Little children like Fujio were starting to think of dead people the way they might think of a dead ant. Such children couldn't possibly learn what a solemn thing death is; they lost all respect for the dead.

And not only the children. Even adults began making disrespectful jokes about the dead. There was one ugly joke about watermelons. Hundreds, perhaps even thou-

123

sands, of corpses lay in the fields around town, the ground completely covered by them in some places. They were already swollen round, and looked a little like watermelons in a patch; and some people were saying as a joke, "If only they were watermelons you could eat them."

In an atom-bomb war, I realized, there were just too many dead people; there weren't enough living ones to take care of the dead. They had to leave the bodies where they were. People got used to seeing corpses lying around, they came to take it as perfectly natural; they came to joke about it.

The next morning, the thirteenth, I again took Hatsue over to the school, which the relief squad was using as an emergency hospital—it was a concrete building and not too badly damaged. They had put the more serious cases on the floors inside, the new cases that came along were simply lined up in rows around the yard out front, along with those who had died during the night. What a sight, the living and the dead lying side by side!— people with layers of skin burned away, people with bones broken, people with arms or legs missing, people smeared all over with blood, diarrhea cases, pregnant women. . . . Some, I could see, had gone out of their minds. Some were writhing in pain. Some sprawled on their bellies, propped up on their elbows with their arms rigid, unmoving. Some were moaning, others were quiet. . . .

We had a long wait and finally it came Hatsue's turn. She fainted while they were examining her. They moved her into one of the classrooms, which they were using as wards, and put her on the floor, for there weren't any beds. They examined Isamu and myself too. The doctor said the reason I couldn't move my left arm was that a nerve must have been torn. They gave me some more boracic-acid powder, though I still had what they'd given me the day before.

The day of the fourteenth I wish I could forget, but I can't. The more I try to forget it the more I can't.

Isamu was without the least bit of strength. Fujio and I took him back to be examined again, and though it was only a hundred yards or so we needed a half-hour. He had to sit down on the ground at least ten times.

The doctors and nurses were staggering around. They had been working without sleep or rest for five days. I left Isamu with a nurse and went upstairs to see Hatsue. I had to hold my nose—regular streams of filth were pouring down the stairs and I had to hop from one clear spot to another. Some of the people on the second floor were on the point of death, and had no control over their functions; many had thrown up on the concrete floor, and the whole place was one foul pool. The patients lying on the floor were bathed in it. It poured over the floor and down the stairs.

I just had to get Hatsue out of there. The woman lying on her right was dead, the body already cold, and the woman on her left was unconscious and about to die. I had to get Hatsue out, but I knew I couldn't do it by myself. Finally I sent Fujio to get Mr. Fujita, who came right away and helped me move Hatsue back to the shelter.

When the sun got low I decided to take Hatsue and Isamu up to the Konishi house. I knew it was bad for them to stay in the shelter, with the floor always cold and damp after sunset. I got the idea of taking them up to the ruins of the Konishi house and making a sort of lean-to. I could use part of the wall still standing and take some of the broken planks lying around and make a roof. Then Hatsue and Isamu would be able to sleep there and get some fresh air that way, which would be good for them.

Though I knew it would be hard to get Hatsue up there, I couldn't bother Mr. Fujita again; he'd got his clothes soiled helping me move her in the morning. So there was only little Fujio to help me. Hatsue struggled to stay on her feet. I got on her left where I could help her with my good arm, and Fujio held her on the other side, and that way we went. It was slow; she had to stop and rest every few steps. But she wanted to go. She knew her end was near. She had said, "I want to be where I can see Kimiyo's grave."

But Takahashi was standing out in front and he wouldn't let us come near. He said "She has dysentery, hasn't she? Take her away, it's contagious." So we had to go back again.

It wasn't dysentery. Fujio and I would have caught it if it had been; we'd been sleeping right next to her. It was the disease of the atom bomb. I tried not to hate Takahashi but I couldn't help it.

All of a sudden Hatsue complained of pains in her belly. She groaned, "Oh, oh!" then she gasped, "The baby must be coming!" I rushed out to find a midwife, but what chance was there of that? I was all panicky; I thought I wouldn't know what to do myself because I'd never had any children.

I stood there in the ashes. The sun was going down behind Mount Iwaya and the sky was red as blood—I was so sick of that color. I was standing there all alone when a Mrs. Yamaguchi came along, she was from Haranota. "What's the matter?" she asked.

I said, "It's my niece Hatsue, she's having labor pains!" Mrs. Yamaguchi cried, "Oh, my! What a fix to be in! I've just come from helping a woman. Goodness, how many miscarriages and premature births!" She said it had happened to practically all the women around there. "I guess the atom bomb even killed the babies inside them! What an awful thing! War is war, but after all! . . ."

I asked, "Mrs. Yamaguchi, would you help us?"

"Why, of course," she said. "Send for me as soon as the pains start again. I'll be in that shelter over there —I've got to go over and help a woman right now."

I went back to the shelter and found Hatsue sound asleep. Evidently the pains hadn't come again. I watched her. It was long after dark when she suddenly awakened and screamed, "Auntie Matsu! The baby! It's stopped moving! . . . Oh! And I so wanted to name it, I had a name all ready for it!"

She sobbed and sobbed, weak as she was. Death had entered Hatsue's womb and sooner or later it would take Hatsue too. She knew it. She kept praying, "Jesus, Mary, Joseph, I commit my body and my soul into your hands. . . ."

Past midnight I heard a loud sound like a snap—it was the child being born. Before I could light a candle the afterbirth came out and it was all over; there was no bleeding after that. The child was a little boy. There had been one big light and this child was robbed of its life before it had even been born.

I saw Hatsue was sinking fast. I shook her and called her but she didn't respond. I could only pray; I put my mouth to her ear and prayed again and again. Then I made up my mind that if she had to die I was going to get her outside into the fresh air and see to it that she died in decent surroundings. But I couldn't move her myself. I kept looking out through the mouth of the shelter impatient for morning, when I could find help. How long that night was!

At last the morning came. It was the sixth day after

the bomb, August 15th. It was the Feast of the Assumption. This is the day when we celebrate the glory of the Virgin, when we pray that we may go to heaven as she did.

Just as the morning light was beginning to come in through the mouth of the shelter, Isamu suddenly raised himself up on one elbow and shouted, "Daddy!" I rushed over to where the boy was lying and looked outside, but there was nobody. All at once the child stretched out flat again. I looked at his eyes. I could see only the whites. I screamed, "Isamu! Isamu!," but he didn't answer. He was dead.

I didn't know whether to tell Hatsue. I looked over at her. She groaned once, and was dead.

Only Fujio and myself left. I couldn't even attend to the bodies.

I had been sitting there for hours, weeping, when Mr. Fujita came by and looked in to see how we were getting along. When he saw Hatsue and Isamu he wept with me. What a slight thing is human life, he said.

He helped us cremate the bodies. He and Fujio and I went around and picked up pieces of wood from ruined houses. We made a pyre three feet high and put the bodies on it face-up—there weren't any coffins—and lit the pyre from the bottom. First the newborn baby caught fire, then Isamu, then Hatsue, then the three bodies disappeared in the flames. Hatsue's charred backbone fell off the pyre when the flesh had been burned away.

Before the fire died down we heard some noise from over at the school, like a crowd of people sobbing. I stayed beside the pyre while Mr. Fujita went over to see what it was. In a minute he was back, crying. Japan had surrendered!

The war was over! I sank down alongside the pyre and sat there, dumb.

All I had left was a five-year-old orphan and the bones and ashes of three dead! For these ashes, to have endured the long misery of the war!

American planes flew low over our heads without dropping bombs, and I could look at the peaceful sky again without being afraid, the way I used to before the war. I could see crowds of people again—where could they all have been hiding? I wondered. I saw some people standing on hillsides, their arms raised over their heads, stretching from relief.

I could see small fires here and there where people

had gone back to cremating the dead. I watched the hundreds of columns of smoke climbing up and I thought of the dead as sacrifices.

That horrible day was four years ago. Fujio is a big boy now. I can move my left arm, although there is still a little pain.

"The Lord giveth and the Lord taketh away. Praised be the Name of the Lord for ever and ever."

How easily those words come to my tongue now—that is just the way it is!

What I'm doing for a living now is digging clams near where the Urakami River runs into the bay at Nagasaki harbor. I've already dug up most of those near the shore, now I've got to go out into water up to my neck. In the winter it's so cold that I cry. But I couldn't complain ever, no matter what I suffered. I've seen with my own eyes those people who died from the atom bomb.

I never think of the belongings I've lost. The only thing that grieves me is that in that terrible time I bore ill will toward my neighbors and wanted what they had and felt anger in my heart against them. This I can't forget, and they remember.

132

CHAPTER VII

Sadako Moriyama's Story

Sadako Moriyama was, in August of 1945, a fairly recent high-school graduate, an assistant at the gynecology laboratory in the Medical College, and a member of the large Moriyama family, most of whose members will by now be familiar to the reader. Here again appear Sadako's younger sister Sayoko and younger brother Takeo, first mentioned in Chapter II; her older sister Shizuko Moriyama Miwa, the mother of little Ritsuko, so important to Chapter IV; and for the first time her older brother Akiharu and younger sister Yoshiko. Here the Tsujimoto and Tagawa families and Matsu Moriuchi, the narrator of Chapter VI, appear once more, together with Sayoko's cousin Fujie Urata Matsumoto, narrator of Chapter IV.

Sadako, like "Auntie Matsu," managed to get to the school shelter before the bomb went off, and though knocked out was not seriously hurt.

---

*I*t was pure accident that I was spared. The laboratory where I worked was wrecked and everybody there was killed, but I'd been staying home for the past few days because I hadn't been feeling well. My house was wrecked too, but I'd just left it a few minutes before.

There had been an air-raid alarm rather early and I'd gone down to the cellar with the rest of the family, except my younger sister Sayoko and my brother Takeo and our little cousin Ritsuko Miwa. Mother sent them down the hill to the shelter on the school grounds. In these raids, some of us always stayed up at the house, in case of fire. Well, we were down in the cellar quite a while before the all-clear, but there was no raid. I came out, and had almost gone back to sleep when Mother asked me to run down and see how the kids were getting along. She'd have gone herself but she had her laundering to finish and lunch to prepare. So I got up and stopped in the *genkan** to slip on my shoes. Akiharu and Yoshiko were just leaving to go to work. I remember how drowsy my brother was— he'd been up till two in the morning rolling cigarettes for his air-raid crew, and he said he was going to stop by and leave them at air-raid headquarters. My sister Yoshiko had a factory job. She went to Junshin Parochial High School, but all boys and girls of high-school age had been conscripted for part-time factory work.

I left the two of them in the *genkan,* laughing about

* The vestibule of a Japanese house, where those entering leave their shoes.

something, as I started down the hill. I could hear
Daddy hammering, putting in some repairs on our bath-
room.

Down at the school grounds I found a whole gang
of kids chasing dragonflies—Mr. Tagawa's three boys,
the two little Tsujimotos, Mr. Fujita's youngster, and
Sayoko and Takeo and Ritsuko and a bunch of others,
running all over the playground. I had just got there
when I heard a plane passing overhead. It looked like
a small plane at low altitude. I shouted to the children,
"Hurry! In the shelter! Quick! Never mind the dragonflies!," and dashed in myself. I threw myself face-down
across a little straw mat and covered my eyes and ears.

I remember the mat wrapping itself around me, and
that same instant I was blown into the far corner of
the shelter. I lost consciousness at once. I didn't see the
flash everybody tells about, or hear any noise, or feel
any pain.

I came to quickly, and my next recollection is of
hearing a faint squeal next to me. I reached over and
felt around in the dark, until I touched a pile of earth
that had fallen from the ceiling. There was a piece of
cotton, part of a child's dress. I dug frantically, and
pulled out Ritsuko. What a relief it was to hear her

135

cry! I wondered if the other children had got in in time, and tried to call them; but my tongue wouldn't move.

At first there was no sound but Ritsuko crying. Then I heard breathing near me. Reaching out, I found Sayoko. She was sitting on the floor, holding our little brother Takeo in her lap. She knew who it was, and huddled close. Takeo clung to my sleeve. Then I got such a fright that I thought my heart would burst.

A little light was beginning to come in the entrance. As I watched, two things that looked like great big hideous lizards crawled in slowly, making croaking, groaning sounds. Others followed. I was paralyzed with horror for minutes. Then the light got a little stronger and I could see they were human beings!—skinned alive by fire or heat, their bodies all smashed where they had been thrown against something hard. They were the teachers who had been digging additional shelter space outside. I heard one or two names gasped, and that's how I could tell.

I began to hear groaning as the others in the shelter regained consciousness. Mr. Tachibana's two children had both been blown up against the ceiling and struck their heads painfully. The ceiling was six feet above the floor. Miraculously, I hadn't been scratched.

I got up and went outside, stepping over the people on the floor. There was no sun. It was like dawn, or twilight, and chilly. Near the mouth of the shelter lay a woman teacher from the school, dead and completely naked. Her body seemed relaxed and her face was peaceful. I remember I stared at her as if in a dream. Four children were lying in the sandpile—the little Fujita boy and the Nishizawa boy, who had been having such a good time chasing dragonflies a few minutes ago, and two others I couldn't recognize. They were all naked and they were skinned. The skin of their hands had been torn away about at the wrists. It was hanging from their fingertips just behind the nails, turned inside-out like a glove. In the dim light I thought I saw many other children lying all about the yard.

The ground was littered with all kinds of stuff, I don't know what, and things were still falling down out of the sky, and the air was full of dancing junk, whirling around with strange noises.

The school building was blackened but still standing. Not a single pane of glass in the windows. I looked in one of the classrooms, and saw pieces of paper whirling around like thousands of butterflies, in the room and out through the empty windows and up into the sky.

While I was watching, flames suddenly began shooting out the windows of the school's medical office. I stood there alone. No one came to put out the fire, even though the room next door was the air-raid headquarters. A factory had been using some space in the school as a temporary office, with a number of women clerks; but no one came out.

I rushed back to the shelter. Stepping in, I happened to brush against some of the men squirming in the entrance and they cried out in pain. They felt sticky, like rotten potatoes.

For the next hour I didn't budge out of the shelter. Sayoko and I just huddled together shaking, waiting for my father or my brother Akiharu to come and get us. I didn't think of anything or anyone else. Yet while I sat there my father and mother and brother and sister were dying. Fifty yards away! . . .

(Later on, when I finally got up the courage to go home, I found the house a pile of ashes and burnt wreckage, and all who had stayed there dead—my mother still beside the well, Akiharu and Yoshiko in the hallway, and my father lying on his face in the field behind the house.)

And yet I just sat there in the shelter. Pretty soon the

injured ones began moaning for water. It was up to me to get some, because there wasn't anybody else able to go. But I didn't know what it was like outside now. I had to be very careful, because if there was another of these mysterious raids I knew I'd never get off with a whole skin again. Thinking that way, I wasn't able to whip up my courage until Ritsuko began wailing. Then it was that I finally made up my mind to go out and get water, even if at the risk of my life.

Outside it was worse than before. The sky had filled with smoke billowing up from the ground as far as I could see. The whole basin, up to the surrounding hills, had been leveled, and flames had eaten their way almost to the hilltops.

The dead schoolmistress still lay at the mouth of the shelter, but on the sandpile the four children were moving, making little twitching, quivering motions. I'd thought they were dead! Now I picked up the four small bodies one by one and carried them inside. But if it had been Ritsuko, I would have brought her inside in the first place, whether she were dead or not.

Suddenly Mataichi Tsujimoto appeared. His air-raid uniform was torn, and he had his left arm in a sling. I called to him, "Mr. Tsujimoto! What's the matter!" All he could answer was a groan. His face looked blank. He seemed to be thinking hard about something. I suppose he was thinking about what he, as an air-raid warden, should be doing in such a raid. He was thinking so hard his mind was far away. His children Isamu and Fujio were in the shelter a step from where we were standing, but he didn't even try to look in.

I left him and went over to the front entrance of the school building, where there was a tank, and drew water for the wounded. When I came back he was gone.

I made several trips for water. I had been at it about an hour when I heard someone calling me from up the hill. It was my cousin Fujie Urata. She came to me and told me about my family.

After returning from my home, Fujie and I took Sayoko and the two little ones to Dr. Nagai's house in Koba. Makoto and Kayono rushed up to meet us. I guess at a time like that nothing could have been dearer or more heartening than the sight of their own flesh and blood.

Fujie started back to find her mother without staying a minute to rest. After she had gone we waited and waited, until suddenly Makoto blurted out, "I'm going to find my mother!" I decided I would go along with him because it was already getting dark—and after all he was only ten.

On the darkening road we met a man coming toward us, groping his way along with a long bamboo pole. Though his wounds were fearful I thought I recognized Sojiro Urata, and went up to him and said, "Aren't you Sojiro?" He gasped, "Am I near the church?" "It's right over there," I answered. "Keep going, you'll make it." I would have taken him there, but I knew Makoto wouldn't wait; he was already fifty yards away, bent on finding his mother. After I caught up with him I glanced back, but in the falling dusk I could see Sojiro no longer. There was no one in sight.

We were now in front of the school in Kawabira. In the houses around the electric lights were out. Candles were lit, and we could hear a subdued murmur of voices mingling with the groans and cries of the wounded. The sky over Urakami was fiery-red, reflecting the ground. It was useless to try and find Cousin Midori in all that. I tried to calm Makoto as I half-led, half-dragged him back to the cottage.

Later in the evening, Fujie came back and announced

that she had come upon Sojiro and pulled him uphill to the church in a bicycle trailer.

"What!" I exclaimed. "Why, *we* saw Sojiro—we met him coming along the road by himself, walking with a stick. He even asked me if it was far to the church! It was in front of the Kawabira School. Ask Makoto!"

Fujie was as surprised as I. She said, "That's funny . . . I dragged him along on his feet about as far as Kawabira School, then I borrowed a trailer at a store and pulled him the rest of the way. Why, somebody even helped me the last part!"

Everyone who has heard our two stories has been baffled, but most people seem to accept Fujie's as the truth. If that's the case, what about the Sojiro *I* saw? Could it have been a case of mistaken identity? Nonsense! It was definitely Sojiro. Makoto was with me. He *saw* him! It *couldn't* have been a fantasy.

Talk about queer stories, there is that business of Mataichi Tsujimoto. As I said, I definitely saw him on the playground. I even spoke to him. Since nobody else saw him, alive or dead, Matsu Moriuchi, his aunt, says it's a lie. She says Mr. Tsujimoto loved his children deeply and would certainly have been worried about them. She says he must have known his children were in the shelter, because it was the one they always went to; he *couldn't* have failed to look in, she protests. Furthermore, his own house was only a hundred yards away, and he could easily have run home to see about his family. She says that he would have seen his house burning, and knowing that his wife Hatsue, who was very dear to him, was there, he would without question have run home. Therefore, Matsu says, what I saw must have been my imagination. She just won't believe it.

The ashes that lie in Mr. Tsujimoto's grave were found in the cellar of his house, but who knows whose they really are? One of his relatives came to Urakami from the country on the fifteenth, and found a charred skeleton with what appeared to be frizzled hairs around the forehead. This man at first thought the skeleton was Hatsue's on account of the hairs. He cremated it and wrapped the ashes in paper, and then went looking for the rest of the family. He found Matsu tending one of the pyres. She told him it was Hatsue she was cremating, along with Isamu and Hatsue's stillborn baby. When he showed her the ashes he had wrapped in the paper Matsu pounced on them, certain they were Mr.

Tsujimoto's. They argued, the man insisting the remains were those of a woman on account of the hairs; but then he admitted he really couldn't be sure, after all—he hadn't looked at the skeleton that closely, he'd just assumed it was Hatsue's. So he let Matsu persuade him the ashes were those of Mr. Tsujimoto; and they buried them under Mr. Tsujimoto's name.

Matsu obviously wants to believe that it was at their house that Mr. Tsujimoto died. She wants to believe that, out of love for Hatsue and herself and the children, he rushed home from the air-raid headquarters and dodged flames and falling timbers as he hunted through the house, until he fell into the cellar and was burned to death.

But that doesn't mean she is certain at the bottom of her heart that those ashes are Mr. Tsujimoto's. I know this, because later on some bones supposed to be his were delivered to her in a plain wooden box from air-raid headquarters, and she did not reject them; she buried them in the grave right alongside the ashes.

But then, she has only Fujio left to her.

CHAPTER VIII

Reiko Urata's Story

Reiko Urata, first mentioned in Chapter IV, is probably a second cousin of Fujie and Tatsue Urata and of Sojiro Urata. At the time of the Nagasaki attack she was thirteen, and had gone with her grandmother by train to sell beef in Mikuriya, some forty miles northwest of the city.

I'm seventeen now, so I was thirteen then. I lived with my mother and grandmother. They used to sell beef in Nagasaki and other places nearby, and I helped them during summer vacations. I was very happy. Mummy and Grandma loved me very much. They were looking forward to my growing up and getting married and having a family.

That day Grandma was to take the train to Mikuriya, north of Sasebo,* a good place to sell beef and I was to go with her. I had a funny kind of feeling about leaving Mummy home. I wanted her to come along with us, but she said she couldn't because there might

* A city and naval base in Nagasaki Prefecture, about thirty-five miles northwest of the city of Nagasaki.

be an air raid and the house might catch fire. Anyway, it was against the law not to have at least one house warden home all the time. I said to her, "Oh, come on anyway, lock up and come along with us—please, Mummy, lots of people go to the country whenever they feel like it"; and I kept nagging her, but Mummy said it wasn't right to be like those selfish people. It wouldn't be fair to our neighbors to endanger their houses. She said she'd heard there was going to be a big air raid that day or the next.

So Grandma and I went and Mummy saw us off down the road. She waved to us from the gate, and that was the last time I saw her dear face that I miss so much.

An air-raid alarm sounded a few minutes after we left, and I was so worried about Mummy I couldn't stand it. I said, "Let's not go today, Grandma, let's go back." First Grandma couldn't decide, then she said, "No, let's go, we've already got our tickets." It was awfully hard to get train tickets in those days. If you missed your train you never knew when you could get another ticket. Grandma said the meat would go bad and we'd have to sell it for less. She said we'd have to trust in God. Anyway, it was a beautiful, clear day, just perfect for selling beef.

146

The train was full of people, all talking about the awful bomb that had fallen on Hiroshima. Who'd ever heard of such a thing, a whole city getting wiped out from one explosion, with so many dead and wounded! Some of the people were saying it must be an exaggeration.

When we got to Haiki Junction it was after eleven and the station was in an uproar. Crowds of people got on, all excited and shouting. At first we couldn't hear what they were saying, there was so much noise, but then all of a sudden I realized they were crying, "Nagasaki is wiped out! A Hiroshima bomb just hit!"

I thought, It's a lie! How could it be? My mother was there! I screamed, "It's a lie! Nagasaki wasn't hit, it's a lie!" A nice old gentleman asked me if I was from Nagasaki. I said, "Yes, Urakami. Urakami must be all right, it *can't* be wiped out! I just left there and everything was all right!" The old man said it was a pity but it was true, it was coming over the radio right now, and I screamed again, "It isn't! It's a lie!" The old man said, "I wish you were right, Miss. I pray your family are safe."

My grandmother was confused, and kept repeating, "What! What do you mean! Nagasaki?—is it true?"

There was a loudspeaker in the station. The radio announcer was so excited I couldn't catch what he was saying, but people continued to appear on the platform, all saying, "Nagasaki is destroyed! Nagasaki is wiped out!" I heard a navy officer from Sasebo say it must be an atom bomb, like the one that fell on Hiroshima.

We got off the train at Mikuriya, and there, too, all we could hear were people talking about Nagasaki being destroyed. I wanted to bite them all—"Nagasaki is wiped out! Nagasaki is wiped out! Nagasaki is wiped out!" It made me frantic.

We tried to get tickets back to Nagasaki, but they wouldn't sell us any. We had to stay overnight; we stayed to the fourteenth, in fact. I remember the dream I had about my mother the second night. She was wearing *mompe* and her neat air-raid coat. I can still hear her—she said, "Reiko! . . . I'm dead!" Then I waked and began to cry and Grandma asked me what was the matter.

It wasn't until the fourteenth, five days after, that we were able to return to Nagasaki. As the train pulled in we watched through the window. It was like coming to a strange country. I couldn't even cry, it looked so different.

We got off at the Urakami station and started to walk home through streets buried under ashes and debris. You couldn't tell where you were, you couldn't tell where anything was. We tried to guess where our house was from the cathedral and the hills and the bridge. I thought, If only we'd meet somebody we knew —but nobody came along.

At last we found it. So little was left—no more, you would say, than a carpet of whitish ashes. Not a sound. I screamed, "Mummy! Mummy!" Just the blanket of ashes, as far as you could see.

I cried on Grandma's shoulder. Suddenly she pointed to a place in the ashes where the kitchen had been. The cement sink and the stove were still there. Between them was some dark thing—I went closer. It was a skeleton, charred black and almost in ashes.

Grandma and I clung to each other as we stared at the bones.

My poor Mummy, to have been burnt to death between a sink and an oven! If she had to die, why couldn't it have been on the *tatami* in the living room instead of on the bare kitchen floor!

149

The sun was scorching and there wasn't a living soul in sight, nothing but skeletons as far as you could see. I thought, What would we do without Mummy? Our house and our furniture and our clothes and our food and all my school books were burnt up—how were we going to live? Grandma is an old lady; even then she walked so bent over that her chin almost touched her knees. And I was just a schoolgirl. But if only Mummy had come along with us that morning! I wouldn't have cared a bit about everything else getting burned.

We walked away without gathering the remains, we couldn't bring ourselves to.

We hadn't any idea where to go. We walked about as far as Hashiguchi, then I heard a woman's voice calling, "Reiko-*chan*, Reiko!" I jumped as though somebody had poured cold water over me. Blackened skeletons were all I could see; I thought one of them was calling me. I was ready to run, but I heard the voice again, "Reiko-*chan!* Reiko! Reiko!"

It was Auntie Otoki, a friend of Mummy's, calling from a shelter next to the road. I ran to her—what a thrill to find someone alive we knew! Together we cried and cried. Auntie Otoki said she'd been away when the bomb exploded. Now she was the only one left in her family. It cheered us up a little that now we were three.

That night we slept in the shelter. Next morning Grandma and I made ourselves go and gather up my mother's remains. We put them in a burnt air-raid bucket that lay near her.

Most of the day we were afraid to go outside because of the planes flying around. I wondered if I was going to have to spend the rest of my life in the shelter.

On the morning of the sixteenth the planes seemed to have gone. I went outside, and climbed up the hill to look at the pile of red bricks where the cathedral had been. I stood there and wept, thinking how yesterday had been the Feast of the Assumption, when we always used to have a big celebration in Urakami and our mothers made *manju*.

Then who should I see but my aunt from Nishiyama, my mother's elder sister! She called me from up the slope. How happy I was to see her! I thought, Now I'm not going to die. She came running down so fast she looked like a ball rolling. I shouted, "Grandma! Grandma! Grandma! It's Auntie!," and Grandma came out of the shelter. They rushed into each other's arms and hugged and cried so! I couldn't blame Auntie for crying and hugging Grandma; how wonderful for her to find her mother.

My aunt had been coming over from Nishiyama every day, hoping to find us. She had a lunchbox with her. She said, "Here, have some of this!," and Grandma and I sat down right there and devoured it. She'd been bringing lunch every day, and carrying it back every night. She said, "Oh, that miserable walk back, feeling so awful, and dragging myself along—with my legs feeling so heavy, and the lunchbox so heavy too!" Then she smiled a little, watching me, and said, "But I see it's going to be lighter this time!"

I don't think I ever tasted anything so delicious in my life. When we were finished Auntie said, "Come along, now, let's go to my house. Everybody there has been worrying."

I thought Nishiyama had been destroyed too, and I exclaimed, "What! You mean you have a *house* to live in!"

"What do you mean? I've always had, haven't I?"

"Yes, but—you mean it wasn't smashed?"

Auntie said, "Oh, I see what you mean. No, we were lucky; we're behind Mount Kompira."

152

"Oh, I'm so glad!" I cried—but I really felt jealous of Auntie again.

Grandma and I were drowsy after eating, so we all sat there a while resting, talking a little. Grandma had someone she wanted to ask about, I could tell; but I could see also that she wasn't able to. I guess she knew she'd only hear bad news. Anyway, she finally said to Auntie, "What about Mitsuyoshi and his family? We didn't find a single bone at his place."

My aunt told us they were all dead. She said, "It was awful. Kome and little Machiko were all right at first —the house fell in on them, but they got out all right; Kome just had her upper lip split open. But she went out of her mind later and acted like a lunatic."

I thought, My poor, nice Auntie Kome! Grandma sighed.

Auntie went on. "She must have been frantic. The older child had been outdoors playing and Mitsuyoshi hadn't come home from the foundry. So Kome went wandering around carrying little Machiko, looking at every corpse she saw—that must have been what drove her crazy. . . . I don't know what happened to the older one, he must be dead."

I asked, "Didn't she find Uncle Mitsuyoshi?"

153

"Well," Auntie said, "she finally found his body at the foundry in Komaba-*cho*. That was when she went out of her mind completely." Then Auntie told how Aunt Kome had gone and stayed in the shelter at the Yamazato School, but she had come down with the atomic sickness, she and Machiko, and Machiko had died on the thirteenth. Kome had wandered around the playground with the child's body in her arms, laughing hysterically, torn lip and all.

In the end Kome's mother found them and cremated little Machiko. Then she got a cart and brought Kome home to Inasa on the fourteenth. Auntie said the poor thing died as soon as she got there. She said, "I understand she acted crazy on the way and kept falling out of the cart."

Finally we decided to get started, but we had barely set foot outside the shelter when we heard the planes again. Grandma and I ran back inside, but my aunt laughed and just stood there. "Don't be afraid," she said. "The war was over yesterday."

Our relatives in Nishiyama were so happy to see us, for they'd given us up for dead. We had a feast like the one in Bethany when they welcomed Lazarus back

154

from the grave. And it felt like rising out of a grave to come from those ashes and skeletons in Urakami to this house with people walking around and singing, and with green trees around it.

Everybody was very kind, and tried to comfort me; but every time I thought of my mother being killed just before the war ended it hurt my insides. I cried all the time and they were sorry for me, but it didn't do any good. They said, "Reiko, you can't bring your mother back no matter how much you cry." They said, "Look at the thousands of poor children without parents in Nagasaki alone; you're not the only unfortunate one." But what did other children have to do with it? It was just between my mother and me. If all the children in the world had been orphans, that wouldn't have helped me any.

Another thing hurt me. I was the only one, except of course my grandmother and my aunt, who really mourned my mother from the bottom of my heart. They all said, "Oh, what a pity, Reiko, I'm so sorry your mother is dead, it's really too bad"; but they didn't shed a tear. There'd been so many deaths that death wasn't strange.

If it had been ordinary times, people would have

gathered at my house every day for a week, and said prayers for my mother, and wept over her, and exchanged reminiscences about her. . . . But now every household had someone dead, so nobody paid condolence calls.

Today, whenever I see girls my age talking with their mothers, it makes me think of when my mother was alive and I can't keep back the tears; and when I hear them laughing together I can't stand it. I believe they're doing it on purpose to make me jealous.

Once I saw a girl nagging her mother and making a nuisance of herself. I grabbed her and shook her. She and her mother were both surprised. I don't think there is anything a person should be more grateful for than to have their mother. When I see a girl annoying her mother, I want to grab her and kill her.

We stayed at my aunt's in Nishiyama for about a year. But all the time I wanted to go back to Urakami where my mother's remains were. Nishiyama was full of happy families and parents and children and I couldn't stand it. Besides, I could see I was getting impossible to live with—anything anybody said, I would always find a hidden meaning. I couldn't take anything at face value. Being pitied all the time made me feel like a poor relation. All in all, I felt I would be much happier living in the ruins of Urakami.

Finally we decided to take Grandma's savings and some money our relatives gave us and have a little house built on our land in Urakami. So it was that, about a year from the time Mummy died, we came back to our hillside.

My grandmother makes us a bare living selling beef and tripe. A few other houses have been built in our neighborhood, so we're not especially alone. We're all poor, so that doesn't embarrass us; and practically all my friends are orphans like myself, so we have nothing to be self-conscious about there. We all wear patched clothes.

I'm now in the third year of junior high school. There was no school for a year after the atom bomb, so I lost that much time and there are a lot of *kanji* * I don't know and many things in mathematics I haven't covered yet. My grades aren't good. We have some students in our school who transferred from places that weren't damaged in the war, and they often laugh at me be-

---

* Chinese characters which the Japanese use in writing, along with their own syllabic symbols. The average ninth-grade pupil would be able to read and write about a thousand *kanji*.

cause I don't know much. They say, "What's the matter, Reiko, do you mean to say you're so dumb you don't know such an easy character as that?" Well, I won't stand for that, and I get into a fight with them.

I used to be good-natured, but now I'm always getting into quarrels. I'm not cheerful. I seem to cry very easily. I know nobody likes people like that, I know it won't do to be that way; but I can't help it.

I want people to love me, especially my friends; but I know that you have to love to be loved. When my schoolmates tease me, I must forgive them. I make up my mind that I'm going to do just that, but when I get to school they're waiting to start teasing me again and I get into a fight all over. The way I used to be I'd have laughed it off.

CHAPTER IX

Satoru Fukabori's Story

Ten-year-old Satoru Fukabori, who describes his experiences in this chapter, was on August 9th staying with his aunt in Nonaka, a short distance from Urakami up on Mount Kawabira. When the house collapsed he was pulled from the wreckage by his uncle.

Satoru had four brothers—Mitsunori, Masaru, and Suzushi, all older, and the younger Masanori, mentioned in Chapters II, VI, and VII. His sister Hatsuko first appeared in Chapter VI.

I was staying with my aunt in Nonaka. That's a little village a mile and a half from Urakami, up on Mount Kawabira past the Sei Furanshisuko Hospital. I was still in grade school then. That was why my mother had sent me away from Urakami.

My brother Suzushi was staying at my aunt's too. He'd got himself a broken leg while we were down at the piers fetching salt water; he slipped carrying a bucket. The reason we were fetching salt water was the salt shortage. We kids were supposed to get water from the ocean and boil it for the salt. But after Suzushi

159

got his leg broken, my mother sent him to Nonaka because he couldn't run when there were air raids.

Our house in Urakami was right in front of Dr. Nagai's. My mother was there. So were my sister Hatsuko and my brother Masaru—he and Suzushi were older than me—and also my little brother Masanori and the baby. I have still another brother, Mitsunori. He was the oldest. He had worked in the shipyards to support the family, but then he was drafted, so my sister and my brother Masaru had to go to work, and they got factory jobs. We raised our own wheat and potatoes and all the vegetables we needed. We had a garden my mother had planted.

I was in my aunt's garden when the bomb exploded. I was standing right next to the persimmon tree. I heard a plane go ZAA-aaooo, like they always did when they let go their bombs, then there was a flash, a bright-red-and-blue flash! Then there was a noise like WHEE-eesh! . . . like a steam engine when it's coming toward you, only it was falling straight down and I thought it was going to land right on top of me.

I made a rush and jumped onto the *engawa*, and right after that came a hot wind that blew me into the house, and the next thing I knew, before I could even get up, the house caved in on me.

I got a nail in my head under the skin. A lot of boards and sticks and things landed on top of me. I couldn't move my head; it was caught. One beam was on top of it—the one the nail was sticking out of—and the other one was under my chin. I couldn't move my head up and down, and I could barely turn it to the side. I remember the squeaky noise from the nail when I tried to turn my head.

I was collecting butterflies as summer homework, and I used to pin them to boards through their heads. I thought God must be punishing me now, for there I was just like a butterfly.

I kept trying to get the top beam off me, but I couldn't budge it. Then I heard my uncle outside, calling to me. He shouted, "Don't worry, Satoru, I'll get you out!" I heard him grunting, and I could tell he was trying to pry up the beam on top of my head. It worked. The beam came up all right, but it took me with it, on account of the nail. Uncle shouted, "Come on!"—of course, he couldn't see the nail— "Hurry up! Out, quick!"; but I couldn't get free. I shouted back, "I can't, Uncle! There's a nail from the beam sticking me in my head!"

Then he came in after me. He lifted me off the nail and carried me outside. It was a five-incher.

I wasn't feeling so good. I had to sit down on the ground a while. All around, everything was wrecked, the fences and the trees and the houses. When I looked down at Urakami, I thought it must be the blood in my eyes that made it look like that. The big persimmon tree was down, too, and it was a big tree.

I said, "Uncle, where did the red ocean come from?"

Uncle said, "What are you talking about? The whole town is burning!"

I said, "How did it get that way?" I was still pretty mixed up.

Uncle said he didn't know, nobody knew. He said, "There was that bright light. Didn't you see it?" He said something invisible came and ran wild over the town and left it burning. Then he said, "Come on, Let's get out of here and get into the shelter!" Just then we heard a plane and Uncle shouted, "Listen! Hear that? More planes! Come on!" We ran to the shelter. Suzushi was already there. He said, "Hey, Satoru, what's the matter with your face!"

I touched it, and the skin came off like the skin of a peach.

After a while some people from the other houses came running into the shelter. Just like me, they had pieces of skin coming off, only it was coming off all over their bodies.

Every now and then planes came over, and every time there was almost a panic in the shelter. The ones near the entrance started pushing to get inside more. They shouted, "Get inside! Move back farther! Let us in, there'll be another flash!" They were so scared! And the ones inside yelled when they got squeezed, because their burns hurt.

The whole night was like that. Some people died before morning. When somebody died it was hard to get the body outside, because we were packed in so tight. That was the way it was until morning. Then we went outside to look around. I went over to the front of our yard to look down at Urakami, but it was all gone. The red ocean was gone—it was turned into a white ocean bottom. That was the first time I thought of my folks.

My mother and the baby were burned to death in the house, and my little brother Masanori died later.

My aunt found him crying in the school shelter and she got him to Nonaka, but he died five days after. My sister died about the same time as Masanori, in Nonaka too. I was only a little boy then—anyway, I was only thinking about my own burns.

About my brother Masaru, we never saw him again. Mr. Tanaka, who lived near us in Urakami, said to me a few days after the bomb, "Satoru, I saw your brother Masaru sitting along the side of the road near Mori. I heard somebody calling for help but I couldn't stop for him—you understand, don't you, sonny? I had to get home to my own family."

My uncle and my aunt went over to Mori, but they couldn't find a trace of Masaru. It was worse not finding his body now that we knew Mr. Tanaka had seen him alive.

Whenever I run into Mr. Tanaka I always think of Masaru.

Then I remember that I didn't think of him myself.

CHAPTER X

Cracks and Fissures

After the first atom bomb had been detonated in New Mexico, photographs of the blast center were released. One of these showed that the ground beneath where the bomb went off had actually fused from the heat to a sheet of glass, in which, upon cooling, cracks and fissures appeared. This was very impressive; other kinds of bombs had never shown such an effect. These cracks in the glassed sands of New Mexico were no doubt soon obliterated by the heavy, lead-packed shoes of the people engaged in the

165

atomic experiments, and by the caterpillar treads of their vehicles.

The bomb that struck Nagasaki on August 9, 1945, was Atom Bomb Number Three. The fissures which then appeared throughout the blast center have not yet disappeared, four years after. I am not talking about cracks in the ground. I am talking about the invisible chasms which appeared in the personal relationships of the survivors of that atomic wasteland. These rents in the ties of friendship and love have not closed up with the passage of time; on the contrary, they seem to be getting wider and deeper. They are cracks and fissures in the mutual esteem of fellow citizens and in their friendship for one another. They are no more than tiny bits of suspicion and distrust. Yet, of all the damage the atom bomb did in Nagasaki, they are by far the cruelest.

Let us consider what happened. When the bomb first burst, at Hiroshima and Nagasaki, the whole world received a shock. This shock was probably felt more keenly abroad, where people learned of the bombings at second-hand, than it was by us who actually stood under the atomic cloud. They learned suddenly, without any advance notice, that a large city had disap-

166

peared in a twinkling, from one explosion. Their horror must have been great. If such a weapon were to be used widely in the future, the human race and its culture would be extinguished, they thought; and rightly so.

We, on the other hand, who went through the bombing, did not at the time have the slightest conception of an atom bomb. As for myself, although I was directly under the atomic cloud, it did not occur to me that it was such an extraordinary thing—I thought it was just a huge aerial mine or something like that. But as the cloud spread and thinned out, once again letting through the light, which had been completely blocked, and it became bright enough to see again, I felt, as I looked around, "The end of the world is here!"

For a moment I kept my ear cocked for the blast of the trumpet from the heavens—so convincing was the devastation.

And the rest of the world, horrified, cried:

"The atom bomb must not be used again!"

This cry was once almost universal among the peoples of the world, but with the passage of time the intensity of their conviction has fallen off. The reasons

167

lie in the realm of physical effects, not in the realms of the heart and mind.

In the first place, the fear of residual radioactivity has lessened. Directly after the explosion, the Urakami area was so radioactive that people who had no more than walked around in it would get acute enteritis with diarrhea. The diarrhea cases were so numerous that one wondered whether it might not be an epidemic of dysentery. People who had worked in the ruins and who had thus had close physical contact with the contaminated earth and rubble, thereby exposed themselves to powerful radiation and came down with severe attacks of radiation sickness, not a few of them dying. And the very corpses of Nagasaki were highly radioactive; whoever worked long at burying the dead eventually showed pronounced symptoms of the "atomic disease." The phosphorus in the bones of the dead had been rendered radioactive and gave off deadly emissions. The symptoms of radiation sickness in these people who had not been hit by the bomb's blast but who had afterward labored in the ruins, chiefly took the form of changes in the bloodstream. There was a marked decrease in the number of white corpuscles. A high fever would break out, with contusions appearing under the skin all over the body, followed by agony and finally death. In mild cases, the resistance of the body would be so lowered that flea- or mosquito-bites and slight cuts or scratches festered and were slow to heal.

However, such examples of radiation sickness gradually disappeared in about a month, partly because the radioactivity of the area declined naturally, but more directly because heavy rains washed away radioactive matter and carried it down to the sea. Fortunately, it was the typhoon season, and the rain had been falling constantly for days on end, causing floods.

The radioactivity did not vanish completely. A half-year later, directly under the point where the bomb went off, a slight emanation of gamma rays from far underground could still be detected. And an interesting phenomenon was the fact that those who had been living in the blast center during this period had all experienced an increase in their white blood count. It was known that people who had been exposed to strong radiation experienced a decline in their white-corpuscle count; now it appeared that those exposed to constant weak radiation had their white corpuscle count actually increased. In general, the health of the latter group returned to normal when the residual radioactivity vanished. But why should three or four cases of chronic leukemia have appeared lately among them, one right after another?

Radioactivity persisted until quite long after the explosion in Nishiyama-*cho* on the east side of Mount Kompira, and the white-blood count of the people there was reported to have increased also. This area was somewhat protected by the hill, so that it did not sustain direct radiation from the bomb; but a west wind was blowing at the time, and as the atomic cloud drifted eastward particles charged with radioactivity fell like rain on the area.

But generally speaking, the effect of radioactivity at Nagasaki was not severe enough for the public health to become impaired, although crops did fluctuate greatly. The first year following the bomb, nearly all crops dropped sharply; in sub-surface crops, like sweet potatoes, there was almost no yield at all. The following year the harvests were surprisingly abundant, but all kinds of monstrosities appeared. After the third year, things returned to normal and average harvests were again made. So even the dread residual radioactivity disappeared without having any great effect.

Many houses, of course, were demolished in the blast, but now, four years after, these have been largely rebuilt. No doubt a fine city will have risen within a few years. People who have been coming around lately to view the atomic wasteland therefore tend to minimize the destructive capacities of the bomb. "Atom bombs aren't so much after all, are they?" they say.

The fact that so many people died does not seem to impress people from abroad. As to why this is true, I would say it is because people nowadays are not very much impressed by statistics. Furthermore, those who come to look around see a city rebuilt where once were only wastes; they see many townspeople, selling tangerines, buying meat, harvesting crops of beans, gossiping and laughing and chattering around the wells, gently rocking babies and drying the tears of bawling children —in all these ways living the quiet lives of people at peace. And thus they think of the story of scores of thousands of people being suddenly consumed as though it were a folk tale out of antiquity.

The world had two ugly scars—Hiroshima and Nagasaki. We thought of these as anti-war vaccinations. But, when two or three years had passed, it began to appear that the immunity against war that such vaccinations should have provided was decreasing. The nations of the world have conferred repeatedly and continue to confer on the question of control of atomic energy, but differences of opinion appear impossible to iron out. In fact, we hear reports of competition in the manufacture of atom bombs. Yet on reflection it is perfectly clear why such a dreadful situation should have developed. One reason is that the destructive power of the atom bomb is now known to be less absolute than was at first thought. The consternation it originally caused seems to have been unjustifiably great. Hiroshima and Nagasaki were supposed to have been wiped out, but it develops that, actually, a sizable number of people survived near the very center of the blasted area. So it must be possible, by one means or another, to protect oneself from annihilation. Subsequent experiments have proven the matter conclusively. The people who knead the strategy of war, therefore, have come around to the notion that even if the enemy uses an atom bomb, there are ways of not being defeated by it.

Had the people of Hiroshima and Nagasaki died to a man, like those of Pompeii, leaving no one to tell the tale, perhaps even the military strategists would be in awe of the bomb, and would feel some hesitation at using it. But since, instead, there were survivors, who reported their experience, the destructive power of the bomb is known to be finite.

And so the physical effects of the bomb are studied, and found to be bearable. To be surmountable. To be not irreparable.

Today, four years after that day, here in Nagasaki we are thankful for God's blessings. Houses are being rebuilt with government aid. We have enough clothing, quilts and blankets. As to food, our bellies are full enough—there are fewer mouths to feed, and much land that had been covered with ashes and rubble has been converted into vegetable gardens. So everybody is getting plenty of wheat, potatoes, and vegetables.

Our expressions are brighter, and we appear to be living happily among our neighbors and fellow citizens in a spirit of mutual love.

Still, in the personal bonds among the inhabitants of our city, the invisible cracks have appeared.

This can be seen from the foregoing narratives of my neighbors. There was the time Mr. Tanaka found Satoru's brother Masaru in need of succor, and made no move to help him. Of course, in the circumstances, Tanaka was not to blame—what else could he have done? No one who knows the story has ever censured him. Nevertheless, whenever Satoru runs into Tanaka on the street he is reminded for a brief second of his brother. This is what I mean when I say that there is a "crack" or a "fissure" between Tanaka and Satoru. Satoru has never once uttered a word of complaint or reproach. Yet the silent gulf lies deep between them. It will not heal for a long time to come, if ever.

And what about Satoru himself? Did he not stay down in the air-raid shelter and forget all about his mother and sister and brothers? To this day the memory pricks his conscience. Of course, he was just a grade-school boy and he had sustained an injury to his head, so surely it was perfectly natural that it should not occur to him to try and save them. Nonetheless, Satoru has lost faith in himself; when a real crisis occurred, that was the sort of person he turned out to be—a fellow capable of a selfish, craven act. How painful it must be to think that way of oneself! What a lonely sorrow for unhappy Satoru!

Sadako Moriyama too lives in constant torment, the pangs of remorse locked deep in her bosom. The reader will recall that she was knocked out for a while but was unhurt—the only one to get off uninjured amid many casualties; but she had stayed in hiding in the safety of the shelter. Her parents and her brother and little sister were home nearby, and it would have been but a few steps to run over and see about them; but she had failed to think of their safety. When her brother Shigeharu came back from Timor, she was unable to look him in the eye when she told him of their parents' last moments. As for Shigeharu, he cannot abide the thought of her inaction, even assuming that their parents were already past saving. He and Sadako never make mention of this—but between brother and sister a gulf now exists.

It will be recalled that when she had come to her senses and poked her head outside the shelter, Sadako saw the four children lying just outside; yet she did not go to help them, for she assumed they were dead. Naturally she was bewildered, confused, with what the world turned so violently upside-down—nevertheless, she knows if it had been Ritsuko she would have gone to her, alive or dead. It was only because Ritsuko wanted water that she discovered the children were still alive.

Not that she has ever had to listen to a word of reproach from the children; they died soon after. Nor has Mr. Fujita himself ever blamed her. Yet to this day, whenever she runs into him on the street she feels a sharp pain in her breast. It always brings back to her the picture of the twitching little hands.

Then there is Tatsue. Right before her eyes had been the burning town with her mother somewhere inside, but she made no attempt to dash through the fire and save her. To this day it torments Tatsue to remember her lack of courage. Unquestionably, even if she had dared the flames, it would have been too late to save her mother; yet whenever she hears the story of how Mrs. Tsuchie from next door had rushed into the fire, trying to save her child and getting badly burned in the attempt, inside her she feels deeply ashamed. When her younger brother Masaichi came back alive from Saipan and asked for his mother, Tatsue could only hang her head and then collapse in tears; and she is still in constant fear that one day he may ask her to tell him in detail just what happened. And whenever Masaichi thinks of their mother burning to death, he flies into a rage, and she must listen meekly. So here again is a crack between a brother and a sister, made by the atom bomb.

Consider Masaichi's feelings—his one hope during

so many years overseas and at the front was that he might come home some day and once again be a good son to his mother. The day Saipan fell he lost the fingers of one hand from a mortar shell. He was trapped on a beach where he had fled with his comrades in arms, many of whom committed suicide. But Masaichi was fiercely determined to live. He built a raft, and managed to get off Saipan to a distant islet, where he lived a primitive existence until his uniform was in shreds from rain and wear. To have endured such hardship, to have striven so grimly, tooth and nail, to get home, only to find that his mother was dead! Not that he says Tatsue and Fujie killed her—he knows perfectly well she was simply a casualty of war; but that does not ease his heartache. This is why he is continually disagreeable toward his sisters. He knows, and so do they, that he is just taking his bitterness out on them, repeatedly flying out at them in fury, making no effort to control himself—the atom bomb should be the object of his wrath, but the bomb is over and past; so there is nothing else except for the senseless wrangle to go on indefinitely.

Then there is Matsu Moriuchi, who does not know where her nephew Mataichi Tsujimoto died, but cannot help wishing that the bones she found in the ruins of the house will yet turn out to be his. This is how she wills it to have been: Mataichi, immediately the bomb went off, became anxious about those he loved, and scrambled through the fire to get to his house. There, while looking for his family, he accidentally tumbled into the air-raid shelter—this stunned him, and as the flames enveloped him he died, with the names of Matsu and his wife and children on his lips. The old lady does not want to believe Sadako's story about coming upon Mataichi wandering around the school playground in a daze. According to her picture of Mataichi as a loving nephew and husband and father, he could not conceivably have failed to think of his family, and when Sadako says such things about him she is besmirching his last moments. But Sadako insists that she saw him on the playground—"and when I say I saw something, I can't stand to have anybody tell me I'm lying!"

But Sadako also said she ran into Sojiro Urata toward evening, at a moment when Fujie was definitely struggling with the bicycle trailer, pulling the wounded Sojiro uphill to the church in Koba. When she found this out it was a shock to Sadako. It made her lose confidence in her mental soundness during those grim days. And because her story about Sojiro appears to be erroneous, she has begun to have doubts about the Mataichi story—she finds herself wondering whether what she saw were indeed a reality or merely a figment of her imagination, and whether the days following the bombing were not one long horrible fantasy.

As for myself, I am convinced that the Mataichi whom Sadako saw was a reality and not a phantom. As I see it, he was torn between his sense of duty as an air-raid warden and his private feelings toward his wife and children. Since the situation all around him was such that there was precious little a single individual could do, no doubt he simply wandered around in a state of indecision: should he make a dash for home? or must he stay on the job, however ineffectual he would be in his official capacity? Finally he must have decided to try and get in touch with air-raid headquarters at the City Hall, and died in the attempt.

I offer this explanation because I found myself in just such a dilemma on that day.

Immediately after the bomb went off, those who were not disabled fell into two classes: one, the people who stayed right where they were; the other, those who took instant flight. Those who stayed on the spot to help stricken friends or to save their home or the office or factory where they worked, were promptly enveloped in the flames along with whomever or whatever they had hoped to save. Right behind the college hospital the ground rises into a hill, so those of us who stayed where we were, were able to take refuge up the hill when the fire began to close in on us. That was how, like my neighbors who tell their stories in this book, I happened to escape alive. But people in the heart of town, if they tarried the briefest instant, lost whatever chance they might have had to escape; and those who did take flight met quick death if they dared stop to help anyone on the way.

In general, then, those who survived the atom bomb were the people who ignored their friends crying out *in extremis;* or who shook off wounded neighbors who clung to them, pleading to be saved; or who left behind records and files, however important, at the office where they worked, the goods in their shop, the tools in their factory—anything for which they were officially responsible; or, finally, if they had happened to be at home, who abandoned their most treasured household articles. In short, those who survived the bomb were, if not merely lucky, in a greater or lesser degree selfish, self-centered, guided by instinct and not civilization . . . and we know it, we who have survived. Knowing it is a dull ache without surcease.

Where does duty lie—in the clerk who preserves office records before rushing to his family?—in Mataichi, who went to discharge an official obligation he knew was probably pointless?—in me?

I was an officer of the College First Aid and Rescue Committee, and I was so conscious of my position, so concerned about doing what I felt was expected of me *as* an officer of the Rescue Committee, that it was over two full days before I got to my home, where my wife lay dead. I discharged my responsibility. What will be my reward in the eyes of Makoto and Kayano when they are grown?

Right after the great flash I was hurled by the blast and buried in pitch blackness under a pile of debris and rubble. My first dazed feeling was a consciousness of being alive, a savage will to stay alive: "I'm still here! I'm alive! Death must be near! How can I escape the hand of Death?" My next thought was of my wife:

"She's at home. Is she all right? How has it fared with her?" Then: "If Midori and I die, what will become of the youngsters, how will they get along?"

It was only then that I thought about the students and nurses and my friends at the college. And by the time I got around to being concerned for the patients, the sky had cleared appreciably and I had begun to feel I was going to come out of it with a whole skin. . . . There is no question, in my case, of the order of duty for which *instinct* assigned the priorities.

With the members of my first-aid squad around me, I stayed at the hospital and directed the rescue of the patients. It appeared as if I were perfectly oblivious of myself—I was rendering unselfish service to others, quite as I had always said I would—and afterward I was praised for it by everybody. But inside me, very different feelings were operating. I wanted to run home to my wife. In fact, as I carried one unconscious woman to safety, out of reach of the fire, my thoughts flew to my wife and I became utterly distraught. But I was out to win praise from everybody—I wanted to be called a hero for saving people from the very thick of the blaze without showing my private feelings; *that*

182

was why I kept at it. I was after recognition, so people would say about me, "He did his duty!" Actually, I took no more risks than such recognition would require.

The young students and nurses knew no such vanity. There was no showing off on their part. They kept going back into the danger zone with the one thought of rescuing the patients and their friends and colleagues who had been injured or who had succumbed to the smoke. I, who was supervising them, who received the credit—I was the uncertain one.

Finally the flames ate into the internal-disease wards. There was one last patient trapped in Ward One, and some of the nurses started to dash in to save her. I held them back.

"Doctor, there's somebody in that ward! Listen! She's calling! Let us go, please!"

"No, it's too dangerous! If you went in you wouldn't come out!"

"Yes, but, Doctor, if we just leave her, she'll be burned to death!"

"It's too late, there's nothing to be done! I'll take the responsibility!" I turned and shouted an order, "Cease all rescue work immediately!" Then, "Come on! We're already surrounded on three sides by the fire! There won't be any oxygen! We'll drop! Hurry! Everybody up the hill!"

Ignoring the cries from the window of the ward, I gathered the squad together and we abandoned the hospital. It was like fleeing along a path in a red jungle. The roaring flames leaped high. They towered over us, swaying and fluttering in the wind, raining down showers of sparks on our heads. Here and there we came upon students and nurses who had collapsed. We picked them up and carried them a short distance up the hill, where the fire could not get to them. I kept hurrying everybody—I was very nervous about the Roentgen storeroom. It was on the top floor of the hospital, the fourth, but the fire was already close. The storeroom was crammed with X-ray films from as far back as thirty years, and the fumes would be deadly when it blew up.

There was one nurse who appeared to have sustained only slight injuries, but who had slumped over in a state of utter exhaustion. She plucked at my sleeve, pleading to be carried. I shook her off. "Surely you can walk, you're barely hurt at all. Come on, the gas will get us if we don't hurry! We've lots worse cases than you to help." I made her straighten up and walk. But it wasn't her trivial wounds that had weakened her—it was the radiation she had absorbed. Several of the nurses were acting the same way. I allowed them no help. These girls were all far sicker than they looked —some were actually in the death agony—and, not knowing it, I made them all stand up and walk without help. I often wonder what their families, and the family of the patient in Ward One, think of me now.

When we had got about two hundred yards from the hospital, the Roentgen storeroom blew up.

My right temporal artery had been cut and I had lost a lot of blood; finally I collapsed. Professor Shirabe of Surgery treated the wound and took some sutures to stop the bleeding, and I seem to have passed out for a few moments. When I came to, I found myself lying on the grass, looking up at the whirling vortex of the atomic cloud. I gritted my teeth against the throbbing pain of the wound, and again my thoughts flew to my wife. If she were alive, she should be getting here about now. In previous air raids she had always been anxious about me and come running to the college. Only today had she not come. She must be dead, I knew. I was oppressed with an unendurable loneliness. As I lay there in the grass, looking up at the ugly sky, there was a faint smell of wild chrysanthemum. Alongside my cheek stood a torn, flowerless stem.

Why did it not occur to me to go to her then, as I lay there in the grass? Was it right to keep waiting for her to come to me? Well, it was of course my duty to stay—there was plenty for me to do—so I suppose it can be said that I was doing the right thing in not going to her. But to this day, when I think of her lying in the burning house, it still tears at my heart.

The next morning, from the hill of the college, I saw the ruins of my home. Urakami was a blanket of white ashes. At first I was unable to locate my house, but, using the Yamazato Elementary School as a landmark and figuring from the stone steps of the school building, I was finally able to make out the stone wall near where my house had been. In the bright morning light not a thing moved, anywhere. The very thought left me weak all over. I was no good for work all day. I just stayed in the shelter. It was but a half-mile to the ruined house, so it would have been possible for me to go there, even if only for a few moments. Of course, I had lost blood and absorbed radiation, but if I had been burning with love toward my family and my neighbors, I would have managed to get to them even if I had had to drag myself. My wife was already dead, as it happened, but in the air-raid shelter of the *tonarigumi* old Matsu Moriuchi, the Tagawa child, and others lay injured, waiting for a doctor. Or more to the point, they were waiting for *me*. "We needn't worry, Dr. Nagai belongs to our *tonarigumi*. We'll be well taken care of in an air raid"—that was what they had always used to say.

Ever since that day there has been a crack between me and the other members of the *tonarigumi*, although we never talk about it.

And why didn't I go to them on that morning? Simply because I was in fear of another bomb. The first one had taken us completely by surprise—our first inkling had been those brilliant flashes in the sky. Any instant now there might be another great flash overhead. I was shaking with fear: that was what made me unable even to set foot outside the shelter. That was why I couldn't get up the nerve to cut across the shelterless wastes to the ruins of my house. . . .

This quality of desperate fear will typify people in an atomic war. With atom bombs, there is no relaxation, even for a second. We were paralyzed by constant dread. Human activities stopped dead.

Fortunately, the war ended shortly after our experience. If it had continued, we would all have gone mad from ceaseless anxiety.

Today, we of Nagasaki, living on in the atomic wasteland, apply our energies to reconstruction. The sympathy of the whole world, and in particular the material aid and spiritual comfort which have been forthcoming from the American people, are enabling us gradually to cover up the marks of the atomic cataclysm and to convert our ruins into a new metropolis, where industry and art and learning and a new society shall flower in the spirit of peace. . . . Does it seem, then, that the deadly work of an atom bomb can be repaired?

Moreover, we know that, in the nations of the world since that time, scientists have studied the effects and the after-effects of the atom bomb. They have held experiments, analyzed the results. They have carefully weighed what happened to Hiroshima, and to us of Nagasaki. What they learned they have passed on to the councils of the generals and statesmen.

And by this the conferences to free the world of atomic menace succeed or fail, and I understand they have failed; by this the decision to use or not to use the bomb is made, and I hear they do not regard it as so fearful, so unusable. . . . A city cannot be obliterated wholly. . . . Not everyone dies. . . . Radioactivity in time is dissipated. . . . It is just another weapon, with greater physical effects than those which preceded it.

Greater physical effects! . . . Do they understand, have they investigated what it does to the heart and conscience and mind of those who survive? Do they have any knowledge of our society of spiritual bankrupts, now striving lamely to function as a community?

We of Nagasaki, who survive, cannot escape the heart-rending, remorseful memories.

We know what only one atom bomb can do to plunge decent people into a pit of sorrow.

We carry deep in our hearts, every one of us, stubborn, unhealing wounds. When we are alone we brood upon them, and when we see our neighbors we are again reminded of them; theirs as well as ours.

It is this spiritual wreckage, which the visitor to Nagasaki's wastes does not see, that is indeed beyond repair.